ASK THE
Angels

ROSEMARY ELLEN GUILEY, Ph.D.

ASK THE
Angels

How to bring angelic
wisdom into your life

Element
An Imprint of HarperCollins*Publishers*
77–85 Fulham Palace Road,
Hammersmith, London W6 8JB

The website address is: www.thorsonselement.com

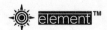

and Element are trademarks of HarperCollins*Publishers* Ltd

First published by Element 2003

1 3 5 7 9 10 8 6 4 2

© Visionary Living, Inc. 2003

Visionary Living Inc. asserts the moral right
to be identified as the author of this work

A catalogue record of this book is
available from the British Library

ISBN 0 00 715130 6

Printed and bound in Great Britain by
Clays Ltd, St Ives plc

For Norma, Judy and Eddie

Contents

Angel of Hope – The Angel of Joy – The Angel of Justice – The Angel of Love – The Angel of Patience – The Angel of Peace – The Angel of Prayer – The Angel of Relationships – The Angel of Release – The Angel of Solutions – The Angel of Strength – The Angel of Thanksgiving – The Angel of Truth – The Angel of Will – The Angel of Words

About the Author

Rosemary Ellen Guiley, Ph.D. is a best-selling author whose work is devoted to helping others achieve their goals and find fulfilment in their lives, creativity and work through 'visionary living'. She is president of her own company, Visionary Living, Inc. Ms Guiley presents workshops and seminars on a wide range of spiritual and self-help topics such as working with the angelic realm, developing the intuition, understanding dreams, and deepening the spiritual path through prayer and meditation.

Her other books published by Thorsons are *An Angel in Your Pocket*, *A Miracle in Your Pocket*, *The Alchemical Tarot* and *The Angels Tarot*. In addition, Ms Guiley has authored other books on other subjects, including dreams, intuition, prayer, mysticism and mystical experience, saints, angels, ghosts, sacred sites and more. Her work has been translated into 13 languages, selected by major book clubs and cited for excellence.

Ms Guiley lives with her husband, Tom, in Arnold, Maryland, USA.

Her website is at http://www.visionaryliving.com.

Acknowledgements

The meditation for the Angel of Love was inspired by the bioenergy healing I learned from Mietek and Margaret Wirkus. The meditation for the Angel of Healing was inspired by my good friend, Rev. Jayne Howard-Feldman.

Angels All Around Us

Angels are real beings of awesome power and mystery. They are God's messengers, whose role is to keep us attuned to the heart of God. Through this attunement divine love flows freely and we are protected, comforted, guided and redeemed.

Angels are part of a large community of intermediary beings who serve between humanity and the Divine. Such intermediaries have always been recognized in spiritual traditions around the world, and have been called by many different names. Angels have always participated in human affairs as part of the grand workings of creation. Each and every part of creation has its own supreme importance to serve the whole. Angels have been with us and are with us, even if we are unaware of their presence.

When we become aware of angels, an important shift takes place within us. Our very awareness makes us more receptive to divine guidance as it flows through angels to us. We begin to see things in different ways. We are more open to the presence of the Divine everywhere. We are lifted up to a higher spiritual plane of consciousness, and we begin to live life differently – and more abundantly.

Humanity's thoughts about angels have changed dramatically over the centuries. Our ancestors looked upon angels as remote beings, as unknowable as God. Angels could be helpful – or they could be punishing, if that was how God wished them to act. Angels appeared on the scene when they had specific business with us. They took care of it efficiently, then departed.

Over time, human beings developed a more personal relationship with angels. Our ancestors thought that only certain people could perceive angels: prophets, mystics, the religious and certain other individuals marked for a significant destiny. Today we know that the angelic realm makes itself known to all who seek it. All we need do is ask. It's that simple.

For many centuries, angels were in the far background of human concerns. This was appropriate, as humanity moved through different stages of thinking, growth and awareness. We are now in an era of renewed spiritual interest. We have urgent questions about who we are, what our relationship is to God, why we are here, and what meaning there is to creation and our part in it. These interests act like beacons of light within us, and angels are drawn to that light. The angelic realm is ever ready to assist us in our soul's journey.

As our global community of relationships has expanded, so too has our spiritual community of relationships. We can establish partnerships with angels. We can know their presence, call on them for assistance, and receive information and guidance from God through them. Angels can provide valuable help in all areas of life, from daily affairs to our deepest spiritual searching.

My own relationship with angels deepened more than a decade ago in the unfoldment of my spiritual path. I have paid close attention to my dreams for most of my life, and so it was natural that the doorways to the angelic realm first opened in dream experiences, in which I was introduced to angelic presences around me. I found that the more I acknowledged their presence, the stronger became my awareness of them.

Angels are not a substitute for God, but rather are part of God's presence in creation. Their presence has been consistent since they came into being at the beginning of creation, when God formed the firmament of heaven. Their presence is more noticeable to many today because the angels have responded to the inner calls of a great many people for spiritual help.

The exercises and meditations in this book are drawn from my own experiences with the angelic realm. Working with angels is inspiring and rewarding. I have had a variety of interactions with angels over the years which have had a profound impact upon me. While I have had some visual encounters with angels, most of my experiences have been on the inner planes, where one meets other presences in other realms. The inner planes are where we experience, in a spiritual sense, our own Truth. The inner experience leads to an unfolding of events in the outer world.

There are those who say that they believe only what they see, but the souls who tread the Way of Angels know that first you believe, and then you see the results of what you believe. If you believe in high ideals and in a spiritual partnership with angels, you will see the positive results of that in your own life.

Before we begin our work with angels, let's get better acquainted with them.

The Origins of Angels

Our heritage of angels was born in the cradle of civilization, in the Middle East. The angel emerged in the spiritual tradition of the Jews, who were influenced by their surrounding cultures – especially the mythologies of Babylonia and Persia, and also Assyria, Sumer, Chaldea and Egypt. The angel – *angelos* in Greek and *malakh* in Hebrew, both terms for 'messenger' – existed in various levels of the heavens, performing the tasks set them by God to keep everything running smoothly. The angels' characteristics were similar to other intercessory and protective beings. For example, *karabu* was a winged Assyrian deity of protection. The term *karabu* means 'bless' or 'consecrate'. The term *cherubim* – the name of a higher order of angels – may be derived from it. The male *kari-bu* was a 'blessed/consecrated one', and the female *kuribi* was a protector goddess. The *kari-bu* had the body of a sphinx or bull and the head of a human. It guarded entrances to temples, homes and buildings.

The spiritual world of the early Hebrews teemed with various benevolent and malevolent beings. Angels were called upon to counter the potential negative influences of their evil counterparts – demons – who caused illness and misfortune.

Angels were major figures in the mystical philosophies that developed. The Jewish *Merkabah* mystics practised techniques involving breath control, posture and the recitation of prayers and chants in order to help their consciousness ascend up through the layers of heavens to the throne of God. Angels guarded the portals at every level to keep out the unworthy, and the practitioner had to know the proper names, incantations and prayers to get past them.

Christianity inherited the angel, though Jesus took over the primary function of intercessor for humanity and the way to heaven. Angels still played important roles, especially in the fight against the demonic forces of Satan. The Gnostics, a popular cult that existed alongside early Christianity, had a complex cosmology of layers of heavens and angel-like beings called *aeons*. When Islam was born in the early seventh century CE (Common Era; the equivalent of AD), angels were a part of it, too.

The church fathers of Christianity – the theologians, preachers, philosophers and monks who shaped the beliefs of the new religion – gave great consideration to the duties, nature, numbers, abilities and functions of angels in an effort to place them in the scheme of the Christian worldview. Some of the questions they took up are presented in the chapter entitled 'Answers to the 12 Most Commonly Asked Questions About Angels'.

The theological interest in angels peaked in the Middle Ages, then declined during the Renaissance. In addition, the

Protestant Reformation of the 16th century diminished the emphasis on good angels and focused more attention on the fallen angels of Satan. The scientific revolution of the 17th and 18th centuries further diminished the importance of angels, though religious devotional cults within the Catholic church kept interest alive within Christianity. These devotional cults regard angels as conscious beings of high intelligence, not bound by the limitations of physical laws, who can be of help to humanity – but who must not be worshipped or adored, or placed above Christ or God. Devotion to angels in this tradition centres on imitating them, for they in turn imitate God.

Christianity helped to build the idea of a more personal relationship with angels than existed in the early Hebrew beliefs. The concept of the guardian angel predates Christianity, however. For example, the Greeks had *daimones* – spirits who could be either good or bad, and who attempted to influence us in either direction. The idea of guardian angels is present in the Old Testament – Psalm 91 refers to God providing angels to guard our ways. Christianity developed this concept more fully, as we shall see in the chapter on Your Guardian Angel.

Our Sources of Information on Angels

You might be surprised to learn that most of our information on angels does not come from the Bible. True, there are numerous references to angels and their activities in both the

Old and New Testaments, but the Bible offers little in the way of detail about angels, their nature, their realm or their specific duties.

Most of the details of angel lore comes from inspired texts outside the canon. Of Jewish and Christian origin, these texts are often referred to as *apocrypha* and *pseudepigrapha*. Apocrypha are 'hidden' texts, and pseudepigrapha are authored anonymously and usually attributed to a famous prophet. Most were written between 200 BCE (Before Common Era, the equivalent of BC) and about 200 CE, though some were written even centuries later. They were excluded from the canon for various reasons, including lack of historical data on their origins, divergences with prevailing philosophy and doctrine, and so on. Many are visionary recitals: that is, they tell in the first person a prophet's mystical ascent to heaven, angel-guided tour, question-and-answer session, receipt of instructions for teaching people/ helping others, and the prophet's return to earth. Many have apocalyptic elements: that is, they discuss the last judgement and the end of creation.

Of the texts most important to our lore about angels, the Book of Enoch ranks at the top. The Book of Enoch has survived in three versions. Written by anonymous authors between the second century BCE and the sixth century CE, the book tells about the heavenly experiences of Enoch, a prophet mentioned in Genesis. One day while sleeping alone, Enoch is approached by two angels who take him up into the heavens. He sees the different levels, learns about angels and their duties and also the organization of creation, receives dictation from one of God's chief angels, and takes what he has learned back to ordinary life to disseminate among the people.

Other important angel works are the Book of Jubilees, the Life of Adam and Eve, and testaments and texts attributed to various prophets such as Zechariah, Isaiah, the 'Twelve Patriarchs', Levi, Jacob, Abraham and others.

We also have angel lore in the surviving texts of the Essene community at Qumran, known as the Dead Sea Scrolls, and from Christian Gnostics in the Nag Hammadi texts.

Answers to the 12 Most Commonly Asked Questions About Angels

Do Angels Really Have Wings?

Ancient peoples portrayed many gods, goddesses and spirits as winged, which fit in with ideas that heaven was up in the sky, and therefore wings were necessary for travelling in the heavens and back and forth to earth. Angels don't really need wings, however, to transport themselves through inter-dimensional space.

Our ideas about what angels might look like have been shaped by accounts of visionary experiences of them. In early Jewish and Christian writings, angels are given various descriptions: they are multi-winged; they are pillars of fire; they have human-like countenances that gleam like gems, precious metals and the sun. Judaism allows no images of angels for religious devotion, so descriptions of what angels look like are limited to what can be found in various Hebrew texts. In Christianity, the early church was split by a heated controversy over whether to allow religious images (*iconography*) for devotion. Opponents argued that, since angels had no physical form, artists could never make a true representation of them, but could only produce an imagined or projected representation. After a bitter and long fight over this and other issues that split the Eastern and Western factions of the church, those favouring the use of images prevailed.

Early representations of angels portrayed them as having no wings at all, or only stubby little ones. It was not until the 4th century CE that wings became more or less a 'standard' feature of how angels were depicted in art. At first, Christian artists used images of the Greek gods as models. Over time, the angel became more like an ethereal human with enormous, swan-like wings. In fact, artists used swans and eagles for wing models, and women and young boys for human models.

As for most people's experiences of angels today, wings may or may not be perceived. Angels appear to us as they have throughout our religious history – in the guise of humans, both winged and wingless; as pillars or balls of light; as invisible presences that are felt, sensed or heard but not seen.

Artistic concepts of angels as beautiful, human-like beings with glorious wings serves a good purpose, however. Contemplation of angels in art raises our consciousness to a higher level, and inspires us. We see the angel as a mirror that reflects our own divine beauty – our potential to manifest our most noble nature.

How Many Angels Are There?

The number of angels is incalculable. Many theologians and philosophers, however, have tried to quantify the heavenly host. Early writings refer only to a numberless host of angels, as abundant as the stars. The biblical prophet Daniel saw a heavenly vision in which at least 100 million angels appeared: 'A thousand thousands served him and ten thousand times ten thousand stood before him.' The apocryphal Book of Enoch refers to 'myriads and myriads' of angels.

In the Jewish mysticism of the Kabbalah, the Zohar text states that 600 million angels were created on the second day of creation, and additional angels on other days for other purposes. In the 3rd century the Jewish scholar Simon ben Lakish gave precise figures, stating 'There are .06434 quintillion angels in existence.'

In Islam, the Koran states only that 'numerous angels are in heaven.' However, an Islamic tradition about the archangel Michael holds that he is responsible for creating 700 quadrillion cherubim alone.

In the Catholic tradition, the number of angels was fixed on their day of creation. An early church father, Origen, disagreed, saying that angels 'multiply like flies'. In the Middle Ages, St Thomas Aquinas said that every person on earth had a guardian angel, but that many more angels existed. Aquinas' teacher, St Albert the Great, estimated that the heavens contained nearly 4 billion angels. Other medieval scholars placed the total number of heavenly hosts at 301,655,722, of which 133,306,668 were 'fallen'.

Clearly, attempts to quantify angels have reflected changing concepts of the size and limits of the universe. The best answer to the question, 'How many angels are there?' is, therefore, 'As many as necessary.'

What Do Angels Do in Heaven?

Angels are considered to have several primary tasks:

1 *Angels attend to prayers.* Angels are the messengers of God. They carry prayers to God, and God's answers to supplicants. They convey God's will, and they act in the world and cosmos according to the instructions of God.
2 *Angels attend to every living thing.* Angels oversee the welfare of all things in creation. Each angel has a specific responsibility, whether serving as a guardian angel or maintaining cosmic balance among the stars.
3 *Angels sing praises to God.* The singing of praise and devotion to God is of great importance to angels and to the order in heaven. Specifically, angels sing the *Qedussah*, a Hebrew term that means 'sanctification'. In Christianity, the Qedussah is called the *Sanctus* (which means 'Holy'). It consists of the words given in Isaiah 6:3: 'Holy, holy, holy, is the Lord of Hosts; the whole earth is full of his glory.'

According to the Book of Enoch, the Qedussah must be performed correctly to please God. Its performance causes the very heavens and the earth to shake, and angels everywhere to rejoice with great joy. Each of the ministering angels of the throne of God has a thousand thousand and myriads and myriads of starry crowns, which they put on the heads of the ministering angels and the great princes. When the angels recite the Sanctus in its proper order, they each receive three crowns.

St Hildegard of Bingen once said, 'And just as the sun's rays indicate the sun, the angels reveal God by their hymns of praise. And just as the sun cannot exist without its light, the Godhead could not be if it were not for the angels' praise.'

What Is the Relationship between Angels and Mary?

Mary, mother of Jesus, enjoys several titles, including Queen of Heaven and Queen of the Angels. In some ex-canonical texts, such as the apocryphal Book of John and the apocryphal New Testament, Mary is herself an angel sent by God to earth to bear his Son.

As Queen of the Angels, Mary reigns in the splendour of heaven, where angels are ravished at the sight of her. She loves the angels as her children.

The angels obey Mary; she dispatches them through the archangel Michael in response to prayers to her for help. A story goes that an unnamed Bernadine sister had a vision in which she saw the desolation wrought by evil. She heard

Mary tell her that the time had come to pray to her as the Queen of the Angels, to ask her for the assistance of the angels in fighting the enemies of God and men. The sister asked Mary why she could not send the angels without being asked. Mary responded that prayer is one of the conditions God requires for the obtaining of favours. Mary then gave the sister the following prayer:

> *August Queen of Heaven! Sovereign Mistress of the angels! Thou who from the beginning hast received from God the power and mission to crush the head of Satan, we humbly beseech thee to send thy holy Legions, that, under thy command and by thy power, they may pursue the evil spirits, encounter them on every side, resist their bold attacks and drive them hence into the abyss of eternal woe. Amen.*

This prayer is still in use today. The story illustrates the importance of prayer, and underscores the responsibility *we* have to ask for divine help.

Are Angels Immortal?

Angels are immortal, but not necessarily eternal. Their existence is dependent on the will of God, who is the sole Eternal One. In angel lore, there are angels whose existence is brief – for example the *ephemerae*, who are angels who live for a day or less. The ephemerae chant the 'Te Deum' in praise of God, then expire as soon as they are finished.

Various non-canonical texts describe how God destroys by incineration angels who displease him, including those angels who objected to the creation of humankind, angels who fail to chant praises in the proper way, angels who fail to obey God's will, and angels who leave heaven to cohabit with mortals (see below). These views of a harsh and punitive God have given way, in more modern times, to beliefs in a more benevolent God and to a more harmonious working between God and the angelic realm.

How Many Angels Have Names?

Technically, every angel has a name, just as every thing has a name. Of the myriads and myriads of angels described in Judeo-Christian texts, only the most prominent are identified by name, however. Even so, the number of names (including variations of these names) mounts into the thousands. (More about angel names is in the chapter Working with Your Guardian Angel.)

In Christianity, only three angels are officially recognized by name: Michael, Gabriel and Raphael. (More on these angels is given in the chapter Working with the Angels of the Quarters.)

Do Angels Have Gender?

Angels have no need of gender, but can assume gender in their interactions with humans. For example, Genesis refers to the 'sons of God' – assumed to be angels – who see mortal women and decide to cohabit with them. Genesis also tells of the three angels disguised as men who visit the patriarch Abraham. Most early writings give either a masculine gender or no gender reference to angels; this may reflect the bias of the times against women. Renaissance art portrays angels as more effeminate, but still sexless. In more recent times, we believe that angels manifest as either males or females.

Can Angels Eat?

Angels are described as having no physical bodies like ours; rather, they manifest as light and fire, or as intellectual fire. Nonetheless, there are stories in which angels assume the appearance of mortals and share food with them. But do the angels really eat? This question has been debated for hundreds of years among religious scholars. The accepted answer is that angels only *appear* to eat in order to protect their disguise as humans.

In Genesis 18, Abraham is visited by three angels who are in the guise of men. He prepares a feast for them, which they appear to eat. In The Testament of Abraham, the archangel Michael appears to Abraham to take away his soul when it is time for the patriarch to die. Abraham does not want to die and, to delay the angel, offers him food. Michael makes a quick visit to God to protest that he will not be able to eat. God remedies the dilemma by sending an all-devouring spirit to enable Michael to give the appearance of eating.

In the Book of Tobit, the archangel Raphael, in the guise of a man, appears to eat food with his mortal companion, Tobias. Raphael later explains that humans are made to have visions so that they think their angelic visitors are human, and can eat. He says that angels actually consume *manna*, a special food which emanates from a very high sphere of heaven.

St Robert Bellarmine summed it up like this: 'Angels can without effort and without hands and instruments and in scarcely a moment of time mould a body for themselves so that intelligent men would judge it a human body seeing that it walks, speaks, eats, drinks, and can be touched, felt, and even washed.'

Can Angels Cohabit with Mortals?

Numerous myths exist in which gods and goddesses cohabit with mortals and create hybrid offspring. The Greeks had many such myths. In monotheism, however, God remains remote and apart from his creations. The chief exception is the Son of God in Christianity, Jesus, who was born of Mary.

There are few cases in angel lore of intimacy between angels and humans.

Genesis 6:1-4 tells of angels who came down from heaven and cohabited with women. These 'Watchers' fell from God's grace and were punished. The Book of Enoch tells more of their story. The Watchers, described as angels who are 'the children of heaven', see the beautiful daughters of men and desire them. They decide to take them as wives. But their leader, Semyaza, expresses the fear that he alone will be held accountable for this great sin. The angels, who are 200 in number, swear an oath binding them all together. The Watchers descend to earth and take the women. They also teach humans various arts, including cosmetics, metallurgy, plant and herbal medicine and magic. Their offspring, the giant Nephilim, turn against the people. God sends Michael, Gabriel and Raphael to rectify the ensuing chaos and destruction, and to destroy, confine and punish the Watchers and the Nephilim.

In Christian thought, the angels who were cast out of heaven on the sin of pride, and who subsequently became demons, sought to have sexual relations with people as part of their infernal activities. It was held that good, unfallen angels were incorporeal and unsexed beings. Partaking of perpetual bliss in the beatific vision, they were far above the gross desires and practices of humans such as eating, excretion, and sexual activity.

Sex with angels has been a romantic theme of film and fiction; in many of those stories, the angel forfeits his place in heaven in order to descend to earth and take on earthly ways.

Is It Possible to Become an Angel
After Death?

In Jewish and Christian writings, angels are separate from humans. In the afterlife, the righteous souls of humans can ascend to heaven to join company with the angels – as well as the saints in Christianity – but cannot become angels themselves.

My own belief is that after death people can become like angels. All things are woven together in the wholeness of creation. The spark of God, the spark of the angelic realm, resides within each and every soul. It waits to be nourished, to grow and to blossom. After death, when the soul is free of physical limitations, it can express itself in many new ways, including angel-like functions.

However, one important mystic who was well acquainted with angels asserted that people do become angels – or demons – after death, depending on how they have lived their lives. Emmanuel Swedenborg, born in Stockholm in 1688, was an extraordinary and frequent traveller to the higher realms. In his early adult life, he devoted himself to intellectual pursuits of science and invention. He lived alone, a bachelor not by choice but as a consequence of having been turned down twice for marriage. In 1743, he began experiencing profound altered states of consciousness in which he was transported to heaven. He was overcome with revelations about heaven and hell, the work of the angels and spirits, the true meaning of Scripture and the order of the universe. These experiences, sometimes involving trance-states that could last several days, continued until his death in 1772. They became so commonplace that he developed the ability to be aware simultaneously of the earthly realm and the heavenly realm.

Swedenborg wrote 30 volumes about his experiences and his conversations with angels. He said that, after death, people go first to a transitional spiritual world, and then gravitate towards their permanent spiritual home, either to become angels or demons. The direction we choose is determined by the true nature of what lies in our heart. In either case, we carry on with activities in much the same way as we did on earth. One major and important difference, however, is that after death our thoughts and motives are transparent and readily known to others.

How Do We Experience Angels?

An encounter with an angel is called an 'angelophany'. We have an angelophany when we are in need of divine help and a call goes out from us through prayer, a conscious request, or simply a desire to be helped. Angels seldom appear as great winged and radiant beings. Rather, angels meet us on our own levels of acceptable perception. They may manifest as a visual impression, or an inner voice, or an external voice. They may be someone who appears to be human. They may be an invisible presence or force. They may come as a message in a dream, as voices we 'hear', as strong feelings or as signs in the environment. Angels also influence us through the words and actions of others – animals as well as people.

There are many ways to experience the grace of angels and receive a revelation from their glad tidings. For some people, the experience has drama; for others, the experience is as subtle and soft as the whispers of a breeze. But all experiences share one thing in common: transformation. For no matter how we are graced by the angelic realm, we are profoundly changed in heart, mind and soul.

(More about angelophanies is explored in the chapter How We Experience Angels.)

How Do We Know If We've Encountered an Angel?

Given their subtle and sometimes disguised methods, it's understandable that we might wonder if we've really experienced an angel. The answer is surprisingly simple: no other explanation will satisfy, no matter how hard you try to find one. Our contact with the Divine comes through the heart and the soul as well as through the mind. The mind wants – even demands – rational, logical thought. It wants proof, statistics and tangibles that can be measured. The world of science was born of mind. The heart and the soul seek Truth. Truth is intangible. It cannot be held, measured or defined. To find Truth, we are led into the mystery of God. When we have touched that mystery, our heart knows it.

Those who enter onto the spiritual path through devotion, prayer, meditation, contemplation, study and good works learn to trust the heart. An inner knowing arises. Truth is perceived and experienced, and no doubts cast by any sceptic can turn aside our vision and our conviction.

How We Experience Angels

Angels are around us all the time, even though we are seldom aware of them. Our encounters with angels usually come in response to our needs, and when we are in prayerful and meditative states of consciousness. Angels serve a cosmic agenda. They do not show up on demand for our entertainment.

We can foster a strong relationship with angels and become more aware of them, and in different ways, through spiritual practice. A short daily prayer to act according to divine will or our highest good, and with the help of the angelic realm, will expand our spiritual consciousness. Our perceptions are then more finely tuned, and we will be better able to see how often angels really do interact with us.

Impressions

Most encounters with angels take the form of impressions rather than dramatic visions. We sense a presence around us, and may experience a bodily signal, such as a tingling sensation. We may feel a soft breath or hear sounds. We may have fleeting visual impressions, such as flashes of light or shapes. Sometimes, our visual impressions may be quite distinct and long-lasting.

Angels may impress upon our minds certain thoughts, especially during or in response to prayer. Serving as messengers of prayer is one of their primary duties.

We are most likely to perceive an angel according to our cultural conditioning. If we have learned through media or reading sacred texts that angels appear in certain ways, this expectation is registered in our subconscious, and then serves as a tool for evaluating our experiences. Thus, there are no definitive 'right' or 'wrong' experiences of angels. We all have our own frameworks for making sense of all our experiences, and finding our own Truth.

Intuition

Our intuition is our innate sense that guides us in making decisions and taking action. Intuition speaks through bodily signals, dreams, impressions and signs in the external world. It may contradict the 'facts' as we know them, and direct us onto another course. Intuition tells us when something is right for us, and when something is not.

Angels make use of our natural intuitive faculty for impressing guidance upon us. Many people can accept their intuition, but might be sceptical of 'advice from an angel'.

Angels work to help us discover our own higher faculties and make the best choices in our highest good, not to trumpet themselves as agents of the Divine. To that end, they often work in subtle – but very effective – ways.

Occasionally, we may need stronger, more obvious signals, as some of the following means of communication demonstrate. We may have one or more of these stronger experiences if we have missed more subtle communications.

Direct Voice

In a direct-voice experience, we seem to hear an external voice that is strong and commands our attention. It seems much different from our own internal voice – it is a voice of authority. The experience of the external voice is common in exceptional experiences, and is well documented in the literature of mysticism. It is called 'audition': a clear and powerful voice that comes from beyond one's own self. Throughout the ages, men and women have heard through audition the voice of God and angels, usually in experiences that bring illumination and transformation.

Light

Angels seem to have a fondness for getting our attention through light. This is not surprising, since they are beings of light who travel the brilliant emanations from the Source of

All Being. Light is a symbol of God's goodness and love. Lights that turn on and off inexplicably are sometimes seen as evidence of an angel's presence. One must look at the context of a situation – for example, if someone has been praying earnestly for guidance and asking for a sign, the response may come in the form of a light that behaves mysteriously.

Mysterious, Helping Strangers

Another intriguing way that angels interact with us is the 'mysterious stranger' encounter. These encounters happen when a person is in a dilemma and needs quick action. A mysterious person suddenly appears, seemingly out of nowhere, and provides a solution, or pulls the person from danger.

Mysterious strangers can be male or female of any race. Most often, however, they are male. They are invariably well-dressed, polite and knowledgeable about the crisis at hand. They often are calm, but can be forceful, and they know just what to do. They speak, though sparingly. They are convincingly real as flesh-and-blood humans. However, once the problem has been solved, the mysterious strangers vanish. It is their abrupt and strange disappearance that makes people question whether they have been aided by mortals or angels.

Over the years I've collected many mysterious-stranger stories. The people who have had these experiences wanted to share their stories with someone who would understand and not think them odd.

A good number of the cases are roadside rescues. Perhaps the reason is that we spend so much of our time in cars! In one such case, a group of five teenagers were on their way home one cold December evening from a church event, taking country roads instead of the motorway. It was near dusk. The engine failed and there they were, stranded on a lonely road with nothing but huge, empty fields on both sides. The two boys could not get the car started. This happened in the not-too-distant days before nearly everyone had a mobile phone. The only alternatives were to walk until they found a house, or to wait and hope that someone would drive along and stop to offer help. With darkness settling and the temperature dropping, it was hard to decide which course of action would be the best. The five of them prayed.

Suddenly a figure came loping along on the other side of the fence along the road. It was a man, and he seemed to just appear out of nothing. There were no houses except in the very far distance. The man easily vaulted over the fence. Without speaking, he set to work on the engine. He was tall with dark hair, young looking, dressed in clean, neatly pressed clothing, and had penetrating blue eyes. He quickly fixed the problem. As soon as the car started up, he jogged back down the road, leaped back over the fence and disappeared.

A unique mysterious stranger encounter happened to a young woman named Kelly. Hers was a different kind of rescue, for she was destroying her life with drugs, alcohol and depression. One night Kelly went out drinking with friends. When it was her turn to buy a round, Kelly went up to the bar, where she saw a striking, neatly dressed man seated on a stool, with a full glass of beer in front of him. His presence struck her as odd. Where had he come from? There were few people inside that night, and she had been facing the door. Possibly she might not have seen him come in – but he was black, and blacks were not common in this mostly white neighbourhood. Surely she would have noticed his entrance.

While she waited for her drinks, the man suddenly began talking to her as if he knew all about her and her life. He was kind and compassionate, and he had magnetizing eyes. 'You know what you need to do,' the man told her. 'You're hurting yourself, and that isn't what God wants you to do. There is a reason you are here and there are things that you need to do.'

It seemed to Kelly that time suddenly opened up, and the two of them had a long conversation. Kelly then returned to the table where her friends were sitting, forgetting to take along the drinks. She started to explain about her talk with the man, and turned to point him out – only to see an empty bar stool, and a full glass of beer on the countertop. Her friends laughed. What man?

But Kelly couldn't get him out of her mind, and his words lingered with her. It suddenly struck her that she had been visited by an angel. She took his message to heart. Within a few days, she committed herself to rehabilitation. Years later, she was drug- and alcohol-free, happily married with children, and helping others who faced a similar despair.

Synchronicity

The external world serves as a giant billboard and sounding board, giving each of us constant signs that relate to our thoughts and needs. Angels act through nature, such as in the behaviour and appearance of animals, and in actions of the elements. They also act through the words and actions of people around us. Haven't you had an experience where a person said just the right words to you to illuminate something for you – or even help an answer pop up for you? Once again, these are cases that are probably the work of angels, quietly making use of the natural world to help us.

Angel Bells

The 1946 classic film *It's A Wonderful Life* starring James Stewart has a famous line in it: 'Every time a bell rings, an angel gets its wings.' It's a bit of romantic lore – angels don't really 'get' or earn their wings. But angels *are* associated with bells and musical sounds.

As mentioned, one of their most important duties is to sing praises to God. Many stories of visits to heaven tell of choirs of singing angels and angels playing musical instruments, producing sweet sounds that can exist only in heaven. Bells, chimes and tinkly sounds often occur when we have an angel visitation.

These musical calling-cards have been presented to me on several occasions, and I have taken them as signs of angelic presences. Sometimes angels simply like to make themselves known in this way.

For me, the sounds of angels have occurred unexpectedly and when I am in a prayerful or meditative state of consciousness. Other people have heard them, too.

One case that stands out in my memory was a prayer and meditation session that I was leading in a church. We were seated in a circle, with a little stand with a lit candle on it in the centre. The lights were dimmed. The group was experienced in meditation, and I had led many circles with them. During the course of an evening, we would go into progressively deeper periods of silence.

We were immersed in one of these deep silences, all with our eyes closed, when suddenly a chime sounded three times. It emanated from the centre of the circle, and was loud and had a sweet, crystal clarity to it. I opened my eyes, thinking that someone had quietly set a little chiming clock inside the circle. But of course, there was only the candle. I closed my eyes and resumed meditation.

At the end of the evening, it was our custom to sit and chat for a bit about our experiences. Several others in the circle – but not everyone – had also heard the chime, and were as puzzled as I was initially. All of those who heard it also thought it came from the centre of the circle. We concluded that guides or angelic presences had signalled their participation in our meditation.

On another occasion I was leading an evening prayer and meditation circle as part of a workshop in a small bookstore. The store was closed and we were the only people inside.

The lights were dim and a lit candle was in the centre of our circle. During one of the silent periods, a set of wind chimes hanging in the front of the store suddenly tinkled. Later, the store owner told me that the chimes sounded by themselves on occasion during workshops, but not during the normal course of business. She felt that angels rang them when they were enjoying the activities.

Yet another memorable 'angel bell' experience happened to me during a bodywork session. For years I have had regular massages and energy healing from a gifted woman, Susan, who feels a close kinship with angels and especially her guardian angel, Emily. Sometimes Susan and I talk, and sometimes we just settle into a comfortable silence and energy field. Bodywork and energy healing can profoundly alter one's state of consciousness. On this particular day I drifted into a light meditative state. Suddenly several musical notes sounded in the room, like a music box that played only a few notes mid-tune before stopping. 'Did you hear that?' Susan and I asked each other. Susan had no music box in the room, or anything that could account for the sounds. The conclusion again: angels!

These experiences have always occurred when I have not expected them. Spontaneity is a hallmark of unusual and paranormal phenomena in general. For reasons we do not understand, if we go looking for the phenomena or expect them, they elude us. They are most likely to happen when our attention is lightly diverted to other matters. Perhaps there is some characteristic of particular states of consciousness that helps phenomena like these manifest in the physical realm.

Other Signs

Angels also leave other calling-cards. Mysterious appearances of feathers are often reported by people. Many people have their own unique signs of angels that have great personal significance to them.

Dreams

Our dreams are messengers, and angels appear in our dreams to convey guidance and information. The early Jews placed a high value on dreams as real experiences of the direct voice of God. The Old Testament has many examples of dreams and visions, affirming these as primary ways that a concerned God speaks to human beings to provide direction and guidance. Some of the prophets and patriarchs had significant dreams involving angels. Perhaps the best-known is Jacob, who dreamed of a ladder to heaven, with angels descending and ascending it. Many other Biblical prophets, patriarchs and rulers were inspired and directed by dreams or visions, among them Samuel, Saul, Solomon, Elijah, Jeremiah, Job, Isaiah, Ezekiel and Daniel. Their experiences include the voice of God, the appearance of angels, and visions of heaven. These 'big' dreams were not experienced for personal entertainment or enrichment, but were the instruments by which God spoke to the people; the prophets had a responsibility to report their dreams.

Apocryphal writings also contain many dream visions of heaven and angels. Chief among these writings are the versions of the Book of Enoch, in which the prophet Enoch is transported to heaven by angels.

In the New Testament Gospel of Matthew, Joseph has several dreams involving angels. When he has misgivings about Mary's pregnancy, an angel appears to him specifically in a dream and tells him to marry her, that she has conceived with the Holy Spirit, and will bear a son to be named Jesus. Joseph, in keeping with the time-honoured tradition of following divine directives given in dreams, acts accordingly when he awakens. After Jesus is born, Joseph is again contacted by an angel through his dreams. The angel tells him to take Mary and Jesus and flee to Egypt until instructed otherwise, for King Herod will search for the child and destroy him. Joseph follows these directions; they remain in Egypt until Herod is dead. An angel appears in a dream to Joseph, telling him Herod is dead, and that he should take his family and 'go into the land of Israel'.

Like Raphael in the Book of Tobit, angels may take on the guises of ordinary people or even animals in our dream dramas. Sometimes they appear as themselves, as in the following story.

I met a woman named Janie when I went to the island of Crete to speak at a conference on 'healing the wounded healer'. Dark-haired and vivacious, Janie stood out from the crowd. Looking at her or meeting her in a casual social situation, you would not know that deep inside were many wounds.

Janie was awe-struck at the rugged, mystical beauty of Crete. This was the land where Zeus was born, and the whispers of the gods echoed in the ancient mountains and rode the crystal blue waves of the Mediterranean Sea. Janie had come to Crete to find inner healing. To recharge her soul. It was the beginning of April, just after Easter. A fitting time to recentre and find rebirth.

Janie was a singer. Always had been. From a very young age, she had known that her clear and vibrant voice was a gift from God. Growing up in poverty, it was about the only possession she could call hers. On Christmas Eve when she was 15 years old, she was left alone for a while in front of a big store window. As she gazed into the window, she remembered a Christmas story about a clown who had no gift, so he gave God the only gift he had, and performed for him. She thought about that story and then said a prayer, 'Jesus, I don't have anything to offer you, but like the clown I will give you the only gift I have to give you, and that is to perform a song for you.' And with that, Janie sang the most beautiful song she knew.

Since that day, whenever Janie practised her singing, she sang two songs to God in thankfulness for the gift of her voice: 'The More I See You' and 'Through the Eyes of Love'. Sometimes she could hardly get through them without breaking down in tears.

The pressures on Janie had been many over the years. She'd had to cope with alcoholism in the family. She had suffered from extreme anxiety attacks from her teens to age 40. There was abuse during a failed marriage. After her children were born, she started to drink, not excessively, but a bit too much, she often thought.

Now she was happily remarried, but there was still a lot of inner healing to do. And so Janie had come to Crete, drawn by the theme of the conference and by the exotic lure of Crete itself. The setting for the conference was spectacular: a resort hotel literally carved out of a hillside, its huge, colonnaded marble structure seeming like the very temple of the gods. The weather was chilly and the sea was wild.

On her first night, Janie had an amazing dream, which she shared with me. It was a dream so sharp and vivid that she had no doubt that it was a real experience.

A host of angels descended from the sky and each angel was assigned to a person attending the conference. The angels arrived carrying Christmas decorations. Janie thought that was strange, because she knew it was April. She didn't know the significance of that, but she laughed because she didn't particularly like Christmas, due to unhappy memories of it as a child. She never decorated for it or celebrated it.

Janie suddenly found herself in a grocery store. The angel assigned to her was in the form of a woman who was working behind the counter. Janie approached the counter carrying a bottle of vodka. She saw that she had forgotten crisps, so she went to find them and brought a bag back to the counter. At first she felt strange and ashamed to have her angel see that she had vodka. But the angel was not judgemental and took her money with a big smile.

Then all the angels left, taking the Christmas decorations with them.

This dream had a profound effect on Janie. It made her realize that there really were higher forces who noticed her and what she was doing with herself. She realized that even though her angel lovingly took her money for her purchase of liquor, the unspoken message was, 'It's your choice, but you will pay the price.' We aren't judged for what we do, but whatever we do carries a consequence. Janie knew she had to take control of her habit instead of letting it control her.

The Christmas decorations in the dream carried multiple symbolisms. One was the childhood roots of anxiety, which can lead to false solutions like alcohol. Another symbol of the decorations was celebration. Healing is always cause for celebration. Yet another symbolism was rebirth. Easter stands for rebirth, but so does Christmas. Christmas represents a rebirth of hope, optimism and love.

Janie went home from Crete healed, a new song in her heart.

Angels also appear in dreams to heal. They serve in the same capacity as other healing figures in dreams throughout history: pagan gods and goddesses, Mary, Jesus and other religious figures. Through the Middle Ages, many people undertook pilgrimages to sacred places – temples or churches – where they would pray and sleep in hopes of being healed specifically in dreams. Millions of people still make pilgrimages for healing today, though dreams may not necessarily be part of the plan – consciously, that is.

The archangel Michael was especially revered for his healing, and shrines to him were popular with pilgrims. There are numerous accounts of Michael appearing in dreams, not only for healing but to issue instructions for the building of shrines and abbeys. (More about the most famous shrines is in the chapter Working With the Angels of the Quarters.)

England's only shrine to Mary, Our Lady of Walsingham, came into being in the 11th century because of instructions by angels issued in dream visions. Richeldis Faverches, the lady of the manor at Walsingham, was a pious woman. One day she was deep in prayer, and had a dream vision in which angels transported her to Nazareth to show her the home in which Jesus was raised. This dream vision recurred on two or three more occasions, and Richeldis became convinced that she was to build a replica of the house on her own land. She did so, and the little village of Walsingham became known as 'England's Nazareth', attracting crowds of pilgrims.

According to lore, Richeldis experienced some uncertainty as to the exact spot for the house. When the spot was chosen and the builders were brought in, they could not work, for things mysteriously kept going wrong. Richeldis spent a night in prayer. The next morning, she discovered that angels had moved the structure about 200 feet to the proper place.

The original wooden house has since been rebuilt as a brick and stone shrine. Pilgrims still visit Walsingham to pray for healing and to partake of the healing spring waters there.

Our guardian angels are also dream-healers, as the following story illustrates. It concerns a woman I knew named Barbara, who suffered severe chronic pancreatitis, which created cysts that had to be removed surgically. Six weeks after her surgery, a large cyst appeared suddenly and Barbara had to return to hospital for another operation. The night before surgery, she was in intense pain. She feared she would not be able to sleep, but went to bed and said her prayers. She slept, and had a strange and realistic dream:

> *I was walking along the beach at sunset and came upon a young woman. She smiled at me and told me to lie down and rest. I did as I was told. I remember feeling warm and very comfortable. The woman then walked around me and walked away.*
>
> *I woke up at 4 a.m. on the dot, and knew that my grapefruit-size cyst was gone. I had been able to cup it in my hand before I went to bed. I was absolutely pain-free. I ate for the first time in months (I had been on a liquid diet up until then).*
>
> *I still have pancreatitis, but was spared an operation that night. My doctor could not believe that the cyst had just disappeared overnight, but said that if it had burst I would have definitely been rushed to the emergency room.*

Barbara associated the woman in the dream with her guardian angel who had transmitted healing while walking around her.

A dream-healing also came to Bobbie, a cancer patient who had undergone a mastectomy and breast reconstruction. During her recovery and healing, Bobbie had this dream:

I was in a dream state and a woman appeared to me. She was ethereal and I seemed to sense her presence from above and to the right. She may have been wearing long, flowing white garb. She placed an orange crystal in my right hand – and the moment she did so, an exact duplicate of the orange crystal appeared in my left hand.

I interpret the orange to be representative of the spleen chakra and associated with healing energy. The woman was clearly from another realm and maybe my higher self, a guide or an angel. She gave me one crystal, but the other one came of itself through me. I interpret that to mean that I will get healing help, but I will also have to heal myself.

The dream was very uplifting for me. I did heal very well and people were amazed at how well I looked during my recovery period. I had had quite a bit of difficulty sleeping during the first few weeks after the surgery, but after this dream I was able to sleep for longer and longer periods of time and get the rest I needed.

The significance of this dream is in the awakening of Bobbie's awareness of her self-healing powers. The angel facilitated divine healing help, but Bobbie learned an important lesson, one we must all learn: we use only a small fraction of the abilities of our spiritual birthright, and it is part of the purpose of our lives here to discover and develop ourselves as much as we can.

Your Guardian Angel 4

Whether you are aware of it or not, angels have always been with you. An angel – your own guardian angel – was present with you from the beginning, in accordance with God's creation. It was present with you at the moment of your inception. It will be with you when you take your last breath and make your transition to the afterlife.

Guardian angels are with us from lifetime to lifetime, and during incarnations we have in other places besides Earth. They are with us in the between-life periods, in which we do not incarnate but exist in the realms of spirit for rest, instruction and preparation. We may be accompanied by the same angel from existence to existence, or we may be accompanied by different angels, depending on the needs of a particular incarnation. At any given time your guardian angel knows all about you and about your soul's journey through all of its incarnations. It knows about the plan you set in motion for your present life, prior to your inception and incarnation.

In addition to your personal guardian, you have many other angels around you. They are called to assist you with different things in life, and when their purpose is fulfilled they depart and other angels come to be with you. At any given time, you have a multitude of angels around you. Your guardian angel, however, remains constant from birth to death.

The primary purpose of the guardian angel is the salvation and good keeping of your soul. The angel serves as your messenger, bringing God's inspiration and guidance to you, and as your protector against harm and evil.

Humans are not the only ones who have guardian angels. Every living thing and every part of the cosmos is attended by a ministering angel.

Our Heritage of Guardian Angels

The concept of guardian spirits who provide guidance and protection is ancient and universal. The angels in Judaism and Christianity evolved from guardian beings of earlier cultures in the Middle East and classical world. The most familiar of these spirits were the *daimones* of the Greeks, who became known as the *genii* of the Romans.

The *daimones* ('divine beings') were considered lower in rank than a god, and were said to occupy a middle place between gods and humans. They could be either masculine or feminine. They could also be either good or evil. The good *daimones* functioned like guardian angels, acting in the beneficial interests of their human charges, while the bad *daimones* tried to lure humans into trouble.

The concept of guardian angels is not defined in the Bible, but is described in general terms. For example, Genesis 32:1 tells that 'Jacob went on his way and the angels of God met him,' implying that he had personal angels protecting him on his journey. In Psalm 91:11-13, God 'will give his angels charge of you to guard you in all your ways. On their hands they will bear you up, lest you dash your foot against a stone. You will tread on the lion and the adder, the young lion and the serpent you will trample under foot.'

In the New Testament, Jesus also refers to the personal angels of children: 'See that you do not despise one of these little ones; for I tell you that in heaven their angels always behold the face of my Father who is in heaven.' (Matthew 18:10-11) In Acts 13:6-17, St Peter, imprisoned by Herod, is freed by an angel who wakes Peter up, causes the chains to fall off of him, and takes him outside.

The Church Fathers agreed about the existence of guardian angels, not only for individuals but also for nations and stars in the galaxy. Every one of the faithful, no matter their fame or importance, was believed to have a guardian angel. The Church Fathers disagreed, however, over whether pagans and the unbaptized were entitled to guardian angels, and also when exactly a guardian angel assumed his duties in a person's life – at birth or baptism. Some, such as St Jerome, went so far as to say that even sinners had guardian angels, but noted that sin would repel angels and cause them to withdraw.

This rather harsh view was modified over time by the Catholic church. By the Middle Ages the church taught that every person had a guardian angel. There were no exceptions for any reason: race, age, religion, sex or virtue. Even the most wicked people on the earth had guardian angels. While guardian angels protected and guided, their ultimate purpose was to enlighten and help the soul achieve salvation by turning to God to live a moral and virtuous life. It was up to the individual, through use of free will, whether or not to take up that spiritual call.

Devotional cults within the Catholic community fostered personal relationships with angels, who were spiritual models in a relationship to God and in charitable work in the world. Feast days were established for angels, guardian angels and the three major angels of Christianity: Michael, Raphael and Gabriel. In 1518, Pope Leo X issued a Papal Bull (edict) creating a special office in honour of guardian angels.

In medieval Jewish lore, the *memunim* ('appointed ones') were ministering angels through whom the universe operated. Every single thing in creation would be assigned its all-powerful *memuneh*. Most important of all was the *memuneh* of the star assigned to a person, which governed his existence; this *memuneh* can be seen as the equivalent of a guardian angel.

Memunim were believed to influence all human affairs and activities, and represented and defended their human charges in heavenly court. If an animal or human had been wronged, for example, their *memunim* would take up their case with God to see that justice was done. *Memunim* who watched over places were held responsible if a man injured himself there. Prayers could not be answered unless the *memunim* offered them directly before the Throne of Glory. *Memunim* helped to bring about good fortune by influencing people to take favourable actions.

Our guardian angels watch over humanity as a shepherd watches his flocks. Angels are joyful and happy to promote the welfare of human souls, for it is the will of God, and angels serve God.

Duties of Guardian Angels

Our guardian angels have a number of primary tasks:

1 *Guardian angels put good thoughts into our minds and influence our will towards good.* Although angels manifest when necessary, more often they influence us without being seen or heard. They influence our thoughts and will in a positive manner. If we lead a regular prayerful life, we are more receptive to these thoughts. If we stray, angels will still try to give us correction, but they cannot force us to change if we choose to ignore the signs.

2 *Guardian angels pray with us and for us and others, and offer their prayers and good works to God.* Angels take our prayers to God, and they also mingle their prayers with ours. When we do not pray or are on an errant path, they pray as intercessors for us. Nonetheless, we are responsible for ourselves in terms of heeding the guidance that comes through prayer.

3 *Guardian angels protect us in times of danger.* Guardian
   angels can rescue us from the dangers of the physical
   world, though much depends on us and our
   responsibility to be attuned to the spiritual realm.
   We may have lessons that we need to learn.

4 *Guardian angels reveal the will of God.* The will of
   God concerns our role in the harmony and oneness
   of creation, through the expression of love. Angels
   transmit heavenly guidance through prayer, meditation,
   thoughts, dreams, inspiration, signs and synchronicity.
   If we ignore guidance, we are likely to receive
   increasingly stronger calls to attention.

5 *Guardian angels accompany and protect us in our
   transition from life into the afterlife.* We need not fear
   death, or loneliness in death, for our guardian angels
   are with us in every instant.

6 *Guardian angels praise God.* Our angels continuously
   sing the glory of God, thus setting the example for us
   to do the same.

7 *Guardian angels offer us companionship and assistance.*
   We are never alone, for our guardian angel is present
   in every moment and circumstance of life. We may
   endure trials and hardship, but we always have the
   assistance and support of our guardian angel. Our
   angels do not make decisions for us, nor are they
   always able to steer us away from mistakes. However,
   they are powerful channels of support when we are in
   need of spiritual help.

Other Angels Around Us

In addition to our guardian angels, we are assisted by many other angels. Specific angels are attracted to us to help us with our affairs in life. For example, we may have a group of angels who help us when we start a new relationship, or when we are engaged in a particular creative project. When their help is no longer needed, they depart from us and are replaced by other angels, who come to assist with new tasks.

Sometimes angels 'drop in' on us for events. When I was working on my first book on angels (published by Thorsons as *An Angel in Your Pocket*), I had the pleasure of meeting David Cousins, the noted clairvoyant and healer who lives in Wales. I spent an afternoon with him, discussing angels and their involvement with us. David commented that the room we were in was packed with angels, some of whom were associated with me, some with him, and some who had simply dropped in to listen. My own sense told me so, too. All of our activities in life are noticed by multitudes of angels, who respond accordingly in ways of which we may not even be aware.

For example, the writing of this book is attended by my guardian angel and a special group of angels. Some in the group will stay with me when it is completed; others will not. Some have come just for this chapter on guardian angels. The energy released by the written words is carried and attended by angels.

So it is with everything that issues from us: thought, word and action. Angels are aware of everything we bring into being. The more we advance ourselves spiritually, the more we are able to discern the subtle influences of our angels, and thus the more receptive we are to their help.

In the meditation exercises given in this book (pages 61–72, 121–234), you may assume the presence of your guardian angel, even in meditations directed at the attention of other angels.

What We Can Expect from the Angels Around Us

We should look upon angels as spiritual helpers. They provide assistance, foster closeness to God, and help us in our daily and spiritual affairs. They serve the highest good and the cosmic whole. They will not solve our problems for us, and though they may intervene to prevent disaster, they do not automatically rescue us from every problem. The reasons for our experiences are many, and sometimes we may need trials in order to grow spiritually and acquire wisdom. Regardless of what happens to us, angels are always present to provide support.

In earlier times, people did not look upon angels as personal companions. Angels were mysterious, even fierce creatures whose purposes and missions were seen as beyond the understanding of mere mortals. Over the centuries we have attempted to gain greater insight into the angelic realm, and we have established a more personal relationship with angels. Angels are companions who share the journey through life with us.

The importance of building a personal relationship with angels has been emphasized by certain more modern-day popes, such as Pope Pius XI (1922-1939), who publicly acknowledged his personal relationship with his guardian angel during a time when angels were out of fashion in popular culture. He said he prayed to this angel every morning and evening – and throughout the day, if necessary. His faith in his guardian angel came to play a role in all the good deeds he accomplished in life. Pope Pius XI was a skilled diplomat, which he credited to his angelic help. Prior to a meeting with someone whom he needed to persuade, he would pray to his guardian angel, recommending his argument, and asking him to take it up with the guardian angel of the other person. Sometimes Pius XI would himself invoke the guardian angel of the other person, asking to be enlightened as to the other's viewpoint. Once the two angels reached an understanding, then the situation involving himself and the other person became smoother.

Pius XI's successor, Pope Pius XII (1939–1958), was also a champion of angels, especially the guardian angel. In an encyclical in 1950, Pius XII stated that it was a mistake to question whether angels are 'real beings' – this was erroneous thinking that could undermine church doctrine. He urged people to renew their devotion to angels.

In building our angelic relationships, we still must keep the proper perspective that angels help us become closer to God. That is the true desire and quest of the soul. It is easier for us to relate to angels, because we have projected onto them a human appearance. God has no image or form, and it is sometimes difficult to feel close to something that is beyond our fathoming. Angels are a bridge, a link and a connection to the Divine.

Why We Must Ask for Help

Angels stand ever-ready to help us, but they cannot do so unless we ask for help, or they are directed by God to intervene. Therefore, it is vitally important to pray daily for divine guidance and help.

There is no matter too small to be beyond the concern of God and, by extension, his angelic messengers. If you are sincere and honest in your intent, you will know beyond a doubt the presence of angels around you. Be patient and desirous of the best possible solution and outcome to any situation, and recognize that you yourself may not be aware of the best answer.

When we pray for guidance, we often have our hearts set on a particular answer. We must always bear in mind that the answer that is in our best interests may be something we have not considered. Therefore, be open to possibilities and alternatives. In response to your requests for help, angels will seek to point you in the right direction. You, however, must take the necessary action.

Angels Help Us to Realize Heavenly Joy

Angels are joyful in the presence of God. Scripture and non-canonical texts emphasize that our reward is in heaven, too. Like the angels, we can expect to rejoice and be joyful in the presence of God.

This joyful state, however, is not one that opens to us solely upon leaving the earthly plane. It is also to be experienced by us now, in this life. Our realm and the angelic realm mirror each other.

The 18th-century mystic, Emmanuel Swedenborg, communicated with angels in their own language, which he was given to understand. On one of his many journeys, he was at a gathering of souls where a question was posed to an angel: 'What is heavenly joy?' The question was asked because the souls were uncertain what to expect in heaven. Was it a state of unending bliss? What exactly did angels do in heaven?

The angel responded, 'It is the pleasure of doing something that is of use to oneself and to others, and the pleasure in being useful takes its essence from love and its expression from wisdom. The pleasure in being useful, springing from love through wisdom, is the life and soul of all heavenly joys.'

In another conversation with another angel, Swedenborg was told that wisdom is the love of Truth. Only our inner light allows us to see wisdom.

Swedenborg talked a great deal in his works about the concept of 'use', which he defined as 'the doing of good from love by means of wisdom; use is good itself'. Heaven, he said, is a 'kingdom of uses'. For angels, heavenly joy is productivity and good works.

The kingdom of uses exists right here on earth, too. Heavenly joy, then, is not a reward held out to us for enjoyment in the afterlife, nor is it the exclusive property of exalted beings such as angels or saintly people. True heavenly joy exists here and now in the material world as well as in the heavenly realms.

Heavenly joy arises out of love and selflessness. No matter what our career is, no matter what our deeds are, heavenly joy is produced when we are sincerely motivated to help others – to help them, as Swedenborg said, simply because we love the goodness of God that is in them. Whenever we do a kind act or a good deed without consideration for the benefit to ourselves, we raise our inner light into Truth.

Too often our deeds are undertaken with ulterior motives, even well-intentioned ones. We do good works because others will approve, we will look good, we will get good marks, or we are made to feel obligated to do certain things. The truth in our hearts belies such works, so that little or no heavenly joy is produced.

The simplest and smallest acts of kindness and love can create great heavenly joy. Our careers have the potential to be great sources of heavenly joy. If we pursue our jobs with the sincere feeling that we are bringing something useful and good into the world, we create heavenly joy.

What counts is our intention. Swedenborg said, 'The angels that are with a person do not see his deeds, but only the intentions of his mind.'

If you hold your intentions up to the light, what do you see? How are you bringing heavenly joy into the world?

The next chapter introduces you to simple meditation techniques and effective ways to work with your guardian angel.

Working with Your
Guardian Angel

This chapter features exercises that will help you meet your guardian angel and deepen your relationship, and receive specific guidance and advice.

Meeting Your Guardian Angel

You may already have a sense of your guardian angel through prayer, meditation or a life experience, such as a sudden and urgent need for help. You may have sensed an angelic presence at moments of intense emotion. It is also possible to have contact with your guardian angel at your request. It is in the guardian angel's interests – and in the interests of the Creator – for you to realize your connection to the Divine, and to seek the highest spiritual help in manifesting good in your life.

We can foster a stronger awareness of our guardian angels through prayer and meditation, and by calling on them for their assistance in all matters, no matter how large or small.

ASK FOR A NAME

In the meditation that follows, you will ask for the name of your guardian angel.

Names are a unique vibration associated with a particular spiritual entity. By names we are able to know and summon. The roots of the importance of angel names date to ancient Babylonia, Assyria and Egypt, cultures which gave great importance to the power of names. Because names were believed to hold the essence of a being, knowing the names of deities and spirits gave one the ability to invoke and command them. Great power could be unleashed simply by the vibration of speaking a name.

Your guardian angel's name is not necessarily exotic or Biblical-sounding. The angel names most familiar to us end in '-el', a Hebrew suffix that means 'of God'. This is certainly the case with the 'big three' angels of Christianity: Michael, Raphael and Gabriel. Others end in '-yah', meaning 'Lord'.

The root of the name may be drawn from the function or duty of an angel. The name Nuriel, 'fire of God', is based on the Aramaic word for fire, *nura*. Michael's name means 'who is like God'. Raphael is 'the medicine of God'. Gabriel is 'hero of God'.

However, many of the thousands of angels who are named in Jewish-Christian texts have names that do not end in either -el or -yah. Some of them even sound nonsensical. Many names came out of spontaneous trance repetitions of names and prayers in various mystical techniques for raising spiritual consciousness. Others were borrowed from different cultures and underwent changes. Still others were created out of the numerical values of the letters of the Hebrew alphabet, which had significance related to scripture and to the names of God.

Your angel may tell you a simple name, even a common first name. If so, accept it in the trust that it is the name most appropriate for you and your angelic relationship. Allow the name to rise spontaneously within you, without analysis or judgement. The name may be masculine or feminine, or may have no gender at all. An angel's name may be more like a description or a title than a proper name. For example, one of my angels is in charge of my public speaking. This does not mean that I channel an angel. It means I feel that my ability to speak receives divine assistance through the mediation of an angel. I refer to this angel as 'Speaking Angel'.

ALLOW DETAILS TO COME SPONTANEOUSLY

Allow other details to rise spontaneously within you. You may receive a visual impression of your angel, or you may not. You may have a more holistic 'sense' of your angel that will enable you to recognize its presence. The details vary according to the individual. Trust that what you receive is right for you. Also trust that you may know more in the future. Your guardian angel may reveal more to you, for example as your own vibration of consciousness changes as you progress in your spiritual work. Prayer, meditation, spiritual work and attention to right living refine your consciousness and enable you to perceive higher and more subtler realms.

TEST, TEST, TEST

It is wise to test all spiritual entities who present themselves to you, even your guardian angel and other angels. Angels and benevolent beings, including other guides who may come into your sphere, understand this, expect this and welcome this as a sign of your spiritual maturity. It is not wise to open your door blindly to anyone who wishes to walk in. You wouldn't do this in your waking life, and you shouldn't do it in your spiritual life. There are entities who like to masquerade and waste your time – if not try to deliberately distract you from your spiritual path.

Ask your guardian angel to demonstrate its identity. You will automatically know what to ask. Remember, angels and helpful presences will never try to persuade you to do anything against good. If an entity is secretive or tries to play games with you, dismiss it immediately. If you pay attention to your intuition, you will know when something is right for you and when it is wrong.

BE PATIENT

Above all, be patient. Individuals vary in their ability to attune their consciousness to higher realms. The more you pray and meditate, the more easily you will be able to do so.

If you feel you haven't been able to make contact, the reason probably is simply your awareness. The contact exists – you just have to experience it. Once you do, you can move ahead more quickly in fostering the relationship.

The Breath of God

In preparation for your meditation work with angels – and in fact all your meditation and prayer work – it is important to be aware of the significance of the breath. Through the breath, we take in the universal life-force, also called *chi, prana, mana, ki* and the 'breath of God', which is the vitalizing substance of all things in creation. By paying attention to the breath, we can relax and have deep, restful and productive meditation experiences.

The breath, or Breath of God, can be visualized as light. Thus, when we breathe deeply and slowly, we can visualize ourselves being filled with golden-white light, as though God were breathing directly into our being. This breath-light brings vitality to us on all levels – physically, emotionally, mentally and spiritually – and also infuses us with an enlightened understanding.

In spiritual practice, breath is also an important way to transmit knowledge and power.

The Gospel of Truth, a Christian Gnostic text in the Nag Hammadi literature, describes how Jesus transmitted power through his breath (the universal life-force) and voice (the instrument of creation), which was received by others as light:

When he had appeared instructing them about the Father, the incomprehensible one, when he had breathed into them what is in the thought, doing his will, when many had received the light, they turned to him ... When light had spoken through his mouth, as well as his voice which gave birth to life, he gave them thought and understanding and mercy and salvation and the powerful spirit *from the infiniteness and the sweetness of the Father.*

In the background of your meditation and prayer, keep an awareness that every breath brings the light of God into your being. Over time, you will find subtle yet profound changes in your inner peace, your ability to pray and meditate, your thoughts, and the way you live your life.

The Breath of God technique that I recommend for the meditations in this book is simple. It is based on three steps, which you will see in every meditation:

Step 1: On the intake and exhalation of breath, relax. Release the tension from your body until you feel light and fluid.

Step 2: On the intake and exhalation of breath, centre yourself in the still point within. This helps to eliminate outer distractions.

Step 3: On the intake and exhalation of breath, expand your consciousness into the space around you. This gently opens your awareness to spiritual planes.

As you breathe, you visualize the golden-white light of the Breath of God flowing down from heaven through the top of your head. It fills the body as running water fills a vessel. See it flowing out through the soles of your feet into the planet. In this way, you will be open to the heavens and firmly grounded to the earth. When you breathe out, feel the light expand within you.

You can go through the steps slowly, using as many intakes of breath as necessary for you to feel you have accomplished each step. The more you practise, the more quickly you will be able to attain meditative consciousness – even in three single breaths, one for each step.

Once you are comfortable achieving a state of meditation, continue on with these meditation exercises.

Meditation for Contacting Your Guardian Angel

This meditation, like the other meditations later in this book, follows a template of an opening and a closing, with a guided middle portion. Have a friend read the meditation aloud for you, or tape-record yourself saying it, to facilitate your experience. You can also do the meditations on your own as self-study. Prepare yourself for meditation and read the text, pausing where you feel the need to reflect. The ellipses (...) indicate short pauses.

I centre myself in a comfortable position ... I focus attention on my breath, seeing it as light and energy which flows down from the Source through the crown of my head ... filling my body with radiance ... and flowing out through the soles of my feet ... so that I am connected to the inspiration of heaven and the grounding of the earth ... I then breathe in slowly three times ... one breath to relax more deeply and let thoughts and tension drain away ... one breath to centre my attention in stillness ... and one breath to expand my consciousness to the space around me.

I invoke with prayerful and loving intent the presence of my guardian angel, to share this journey with me ...

assisting me with seeing things in new ways ... and inspiring me to take loving action in the world ... Now before me arise impressions ... I observe them ... and give thanks for my partnership with the angelic realm.

I ask for my guardian angel to be made known to me by a sign ... and by this sign I shall always be made aware of the presence of my angel ... I take a moment for this sign to appear ... a word ... an image ... a feeling ... a sound ... it comes spontaneously to my attention.

I ask for a vision of my guardian angel ... I ask for my physical eyes to behold the vibrations of light that have been invisible to me ... With my eyes closed, I direct my inner eyes downward ... and slowly raise them up ... allowing the vision to unfold before me.

I ask for the name of my guardian angel ... and acknowledge with love and gratitude the name that comes spontaneously.

I receive a gift from my guardian angel ... a sign, a token of our bond ... I am aware that I also have a gift for my angel ... and I bestow this gift.

From this moment forward I know I shall be more attuned to the angelic realm ... to the presence of my guardian angel and other angels who come to work with me ... and I shall be more attuned to the divine guidance that flows from the Creator through angels to me ... I reaffirm my intent and my commitment to walk the path of Light, Love and Truth.

I take three measured breaths ... feeling the breath flow through my body ... reconnecting me to the present moment in time, space and place ... I give thanks to my guardian angel for the blessing of this experience ... and I return refreshed from my journey.

Record the details of your impressions of your guardian angel, so that they become fixed in consciousness. Meditations are often like dreams – the details disappear from memory if they are not recorded in some way.

Did you perceive any other angels along with your guardian? What information was conveyed about their identities and roles?

You can modify this meditation to ask to meet other angels, even those who have specific purposes. For example, you might ask to meet the angel who aids you in relationships, or in a creative or artistic pursuit.

Asking for Guidance

Your guardian angel can serve as the voice of both divine guidance and your intuition. In prayer and meditation, you can ask for your angel's assistance in making decisions, solving problems and difficult situations, and accomplishing goals.

When possible, frame your questions for yes-or-no responses; for example, 'Should I _____?' Simple questions will receive the clearest answers. You can certainly ask more complex questions, such as 'How can I_____?' and 'Show me what I need to do to_____.' We can also ask 'Why?' for many matters.

In a meditative or prayerful state, ask your question and request your guardian angel – or another angel who is around you – to help you receive and understand the answer. Sit in silence for a while, resting in peace and allowing distracting thoughts to pass through you. The answer may come to you during your meditation. Or, it may come in one of the other ways that angels communicate with us, as noted in the chapter How We Experience Angels:

- Direct voice or inner voice
- Mental or bodily impressions
- Inspiration
- Intuition
- Signs and synchronicity
- Dreams

Answers may come later, even arriving in stages via multiple types of communication. Remember that the angelic realm uses the most appropriate means to convey messages for every situation and individual.

Validating Answers

It's not unusual, however, to wonder if you've *really* received the answers. Perhaps you've misread the answers, or projected wishful thinking. How can you be certain of your answers?

As you gain more experience with the angelic realm, you will recognize the unmistakable 'feel' or 'atmosphere' of an angel's presence. You will experience the confidence and certainty of it deep within your being, like a warm light. In the meditation for contact, the receiving of the sign and the gift from your guardian angel provides tangible ways for you to identify your communication. Impressions around these items arise spontaneously when angelic guidance is transmitted.

If you are ever uncertain about your guidance, do not hesitate to ask for validation – a sign that you have indeed received the answer to your question. Try to avoid repeated validations, as you may actually increase your doubt and decrease your self-confidence. Asking for divine help is a faith-building process. We ask and then we must have confidence and trust in the answers.

Our ability to see an answer may be impaired by our attachment to an outcome. Perhaps you hope strongly for a certain answer. Attachment interferes with the intuitive process and clouds the true and right answer. When we ask for guidance, we must be prepared for an answer that may be different than the one we expect or hope for.

You have probably experienced situations in which your attachments caused you to follow a wrong course of action. You received the guidance to do otherwise, but persisted. Later, you found yourself saying, 'Well, I *knew* that wasn't going to work out,' or 'I had a feeling I shouldn't do that.' Angels can only deliver the guidance. They cannot make us follow it.

Sometimes uncertainty can be cleared up by rephrasing your question. In a given situation, we may see our options as limited. If we're looking in only one direction, we can't see the real answer off to the side. If you ask a yes-or-no question and are not clear about the response, try the following meditation. Prepare yourself to detach from your expectations and fears; allow impressions to come easily, without trying to analyse or judge them.

Guardian Angel Conference

If you have a problem that requires resolving differences or conflict with others, try the popes' technique of asking for a guardian angel conference. Tell your guardian angel that you sincerely wish to resolve the matter in the highest interest of all, and request the angel to consult with the guardian angels of the other parties. You should *not* ask for your angel to try to make others see your viewpoint or do what you want.

Remember, angels work for the harmony of the whole. In asking their help, you must be prepared to do your part to ensure a satisfactory outcome.

Ask your guardian angel to convey back to you the resulting guidance necessary for resolution.

Meditation on The Three Doorways

This is an excellent meditation exercise for obtaining guidance on alternative courses of action. It is especially helpful if you feel blocked. Sometimes it is genuinely hard to see the wood for the trees. This will help you get past blockages so that you can see your situation with more clarity.

I centre myself in a comfortable position ... I focus attention on my breath, seeing it as light and energy which flows down from the Source through the crown of my head ... filling my body with radiance ... and flowing out through the soles of my feet ... so that I am connected to the inspiration of heaven and the grounding of the earth ... I then breathe in slowly three times ... one breath to relax more deeply and let thoughts and tension drain away ... one breath to centre my attention in stillness ... and one breath to expand my consciousness to the space around me.

I invoke with prayerful and loving intent the presence of my guardian angel, to help me see correctly the answer I have been given to my question, 'Should I _____?'

I see before me three doorways ... they are neutral and equal in appearance ... Each is marked with a sign over the top ... One is marked Yes ... One is marked No ... and one is marked Other.

With my guardian angel at my side, I pass through the door marked Yes ... On the other side I am shown the 'yes' answer to my question ... Impressions rise spontaneously ... I pay close attention to my reactions.

With my guardian angel at my side, I pass on through the door marked No ... I am shown the 'no' answer to my question ... Impressions rise spontaneously ... I pay close attention to my reactions.

With my guardian angel at my side, I pass on through the third door marked Other ... On the other side is an answer I have not considered ... perhaps not even been aware of ... Impressions rise spontaneously ... I pay close attention to my reactions.

I take three measured breaths ... feeling the breath flow through my body ... reconnecting me to the present moment in time, space and place ... I give thanks to my guardian angel for the blessing of this experience ... and I return refreshed from my journey.

From this meditation exercise, you can sort out your spontaneous feelings and reactions to the possible scenarios of yes, no and other. Perhaps one doorway experience was more detailed and vivid than the others. Perhaps one was a blank.

You may know immediately if your initial answer was validated. Do not worry if it still eludes you – you may need to think more about the meditation or 'sleep on it'. Everyone has his or her own processing filters; also, different situations may require additional work.

Meditation to Receive the Scroll of the Soul Imprint

The next meditation takes you into deeper spiritual territory under the guidance of your guardian angel. The Scroll of the Soul Imprint involves receiving information on a more intuitive level about ourselves as souls. The scroll is a tool to help you see yourself as more than the personality you are in this life. The purpose of it is to broaden your perspective of who you are, and to deepen your self-knowledge.

The exact nature of the 'Soul Imprint' is part of the Great Mystery for you to discover. It concerns your divine origins and heritage and your lifetimes upon lifetimes. It eludes a precise definition. If you do this meditation periodically, you will have a different experience of the Soul Imprint each time.

I centre myself in a comfortable position ... I focus attention on my breath, seeing it as light and energy which flows down from the Source through the crown of my head ... filling my body with radiance ... and flowing out through the soles of my feet ... so that I am connected to the inspiration of heaven and the grounding of the earth ... I then breathe in slowly three times ... one breath to relax more deeply and let thoughts and tension drain away ... one breath to centre my attention in stillness ... and one breath to expand my consciousness to the space around me.

I invoke with prayerful and loving intent the presence of my guardian angel, to share this journey with me ... assisting me with seeing things in new ways ... and inspiring me to take loving action in the world ... Now before me arise impressions of my guardian angel ... I take a moment to observe ... and to give thanks for my partnership with the angelic realm.

Before me appears an immense rainbow that stretches into the heavens ... and beyond into infinity ... it is the rainbow to the higher realms ... to enlightenment ... to the treasures of the kingdom of God ... With my guardian angel, I rise and travel the rainbow ... moving with ease and speed ... stars and worlds going past me ... I enter a realm of timelessness ... and am in perfect peace and tranquillity.

Our destination is a great temple ... which appears now before us ... I pay attention to its appearance ... and notice details ... The temple is enveloped in light ... The light has such a high vibration that it emits a sound ... which has a musical quality I cannot link to any sound on earth ... It penetrates my being ... and elicits unbounded joy within me.

My guardian angel leads me inside the temple ... into a great room full of streams of coloured light ... each of which has its own sound ... and together the sounds and the lights create a cosmic symphony unlike any I have ever heard ... this is the music of heaven ... the music of the spheres ... the sounds behind creation.

There is an altar in the room ... I observe it carefully ... and on the altar is a scroll of parchment ... It is the precious Scroll of the Soul Imprint ... My guardian angel gives me the scroll ... In timelessness this scroll has awaited my coming ... it bears a message for me ... When

I touch the scroll and read the message it glows with divine light ... I am to take the scroll with me.

We take leave of the temple ... and return along the rainbow bridge ... past star fields in formation ... worlds being born and worlds dying ... the unending cycles of eternity. Things shall come and things shall pass ... dust to dust and ashes to ashes ... but my soul has life eternal ... and I am always in the presence of angels ... whose footprints of light are the dew of heaven strewn among the stars ... In the face of change this bond of soul and heaven shall never break.

I unfold the scroll and read its message ... and give thanks to my guardian angel ... and thanks to God the Creator.

I take three measured breaths ... feeling the breath flow through my body ... reconnecting me to the present moment in time, space and place ... I give thanks to my guardian angel for the blessing of this experience ... and I return refreshed from my journey.

While this experience is fresh in your mind, record it in your spiritual journal. Write down the message you read on the scroll, and your thoughts about what it means.

Divine messages are alchemical, in that they unfold new meanings in changing states of consciousness. You can gain additional insights by focusing on the message in prayer and meditation, and by asking your guardian angel to give you more information in your dreams.

On Being a God-bearer

This exercise is a setting of intention through a simple daily prayer aimed at lifting us up to manifest our highest potential. It is inspired by a reverence for Mary, Queen of the Angels, bestowed in recognition many centuries ago by the founding fathers of Christianity. The fathers gave an important title to Mary: *Theotokos*, a Greek term for 'God-bearer'. The title formally recognized Mary as the mother of the Son of God.

As the agents of Mary, angels serve as God-bearers as well, not in the sense of motherhood, but in the sense of carrying, or bearing, God to us. Through their ministrations, they bear the essence and presence of God into the material world.

Throughout history, Mary has made many appearances in visions to people all over the world. She exhorts them to pray and to live righteous lives, not only for their sake, but for the sake of the world. Marian apparitions, as these visionary experiences are called, have increased dramatically in the past few decades. Although only a handful of all the thousands of cases are recognized as 'official', numerous visionaries know in their hearts they have truly encountered Mary.

Like encounters with Mary, our experiences of angels have dramatically increased. Is the reason due to urgency over our spiritual condition, or because more of us are open to visionary experience? The answer may be a bit of both. In casting an eye over history, it seems that humanity has made slow progress in virtuous living.

The term *Theotokos* has meaning for us all. We are all summoned to be God-bearers, not in a literal sense, but in a spiritual sense. By following Mary's instructions to pray and live virtuous lives, we become the bearers of the unconditional love of God into the world. When we ask for the help of angels to do so, our efforts – and our results – are greatly magnified and glorified.

Pledge to serve as a God-bearer in daily life. The prayer request to do so is simple:

'Please show me how to bring your presence into the world today.'

That's all you need say. Through your guardian angel, God will fill in the blanks where divine presence is most needed in any given situation. The angels around you will grace your intention and guide you to act accordingly. If you make this your daily intent, being a God-bearer will become second-nature to you. You won't have to think about it, because you will become it. It will be part of who you are. St Francis de Sales said, 'Every action of our daily life should be

influenced by gentleness, temperance, humility, and purity.'
The God-bearer prayer will help you to achieve those virtues
– and more.

Soon you will find yourself thinking and acting much differently. People will respond to you differently. You are likely to find that life goes along more smoothly. Problems will
not disappear, but they will be easier to manage and solve,
and you will be less likely to feel overwhelmed.

At the close of the day, reflect how the God-bearer prayer
has influenced you.

Working with the Angels of the Quarters

Of all the myriads and myriads of angels, only three are best-known to us: Gabriel, Michael and Raphael, who are the only angels mentioned by name in Scripture. A fourth angel, Uriel, who appears in non-canonical works such as the Book of Enoch, is lesser known. These four angels are the 'power-houses' of angel lore. They are the Angels of the Four Quarters – four anchors of the foundation of the world. They are powerful allies to us in our spiritual work.

Gabriel

Gabriel's name means 'hero of God' or 'the mighty one'. Gabriel is the angel of revelation, wisdom, mercy, redemption and promise. He is among the angels identified as the angel of death; angel of great counsel; angel of peace; angel of prayer; angel of truth; and as one of the angels of the earth; angels of the lord of the spirits; angels over the consummation; angels of mercy; and one of the angels of destruction sent to Sodom and Gomorrah. He guides the soul from paradise to the womb, and instructs the soul for the nine months prior to birth. He sits at the left hand of God.

As important and well-known as he is, Gabriel is mentioned but four times in the Bible, and always in connection with important news. In the Old Testament, he is named as Daniel's frequent visitor, bringing prophetic visions of apocalyptic proportion (Daniel 8:16, 9:21). In the New Testament, Gabriel gives his name to Zechariah – 'I am Gabriel who stands in God's presence' – when he announces the coming birth of John the Baptist (Luke 1:19). He is the angel who comes to Mary to announce the coming birth of Jesus (the Annunciation). Luke 1:26-38 describes the encounter between Gabriel and Mary. He appears to her, tells her she has found favour with God, and that she will become pregnant with a son who is to be named Jesus. When Mary wonders how this can happen, since she is a virgin, Gabriel tells her the Holy Spirit will come upon her, and the child will be holy. When she consents ('Behold the handmaid of the Lord; be it unto me according to thy word') the angel departs.

Gabriel is credited with other major acts of unnamed angels concerning Jesus: as the angel who appears in a dream to Joseph, warning him to take his family and flee to Egypt to avoid Herod's hunt for the baby Jesus (Matthew 2:13); as the angel some authorities say appears in the Garden of Gethsemane to provide strength and support to Jesus in his agony (Luke 22); and as the 'angel of the Lord' who has a countenance as lightning and a raiment as snow, who rolls back the stone from the tomb of Jesus and sits upon it (Matthew 28:2). In addition, Gabriel is said to be the unnamed archangel in 1 Thessalonians 4:15 who sounds the trumpet of judgement and resurrection.

Gabriel appears frequently in works outside the Bible, where he is one of God's most important messengers.

He is the most famous of all angels in art, for the Annunciation is the most frequently painted scene in all of Western art. He is shown holding a lily, the symbol of purity.

Michael

Gabriel may be the most depicted angel, but Michael is by far the most famous of all. His name means 'who is like God' or 'who is as God'. He is mentioned by name in both the Old and New Testaments. According to lore, Satan trembles at the mere mention of his name, and all the angels of heaven bow down before him in obedience. Michael inspires fidelity to God.

His chief roles are many: warrior, priest, protector, healer, guardian, weigher of souls in judgement, and guide of souls to the afterlife. He holds numerous offices in heaven: He is chief of the virtues and archangels, one of the angels of the presence who stand before God, a prince of light, and an angel of truth, repentance, righteousness, mercy and salvation. He is the primary stand-in for God as the Angel of the Lord.

Many people look upon Michael as the 'tough' angel who battles evil with his sword and shield. In art, he is usually shown either trampling the serpent – an image from his victorious fight with the Satanic forces in the Book of Revelation – or weighing the souls of the righteous and the sinners.

Throughout the ages, Michael has been an important angel of healing, and many shrines were erected and dedicated to him for that purpose. Legends tell of his appearances in dreams to heal or issue instructions for building shrines. The famous abbey of Mont St Michel in Normandy, France, and the monastery of St Michael's Mount in Cornwall, were reputedly built because of appearances of the angel.

In the case of Mont St Michel, Michael appeared three times in dream visions in 708 to St Aubert, bishop of Avranches (a nearby town), and instructed him to build a chapel there. The bishop did not believe Michael and asked him to prove his identity. The angel pushed his finger through the bishop's skull. The bishop asked for still more proof. Michael told him a stolen bull would be found at the top of the rock; it was. Still Aubert was sceptical. Michael told him to send two messengers to Monte Gargano, where they would be given the red cloak that Michael wore when he appeared there and had left upon the altar, as well as a fragment of the altar on which he had set his foot. The messengers were sent and they returned with the promised items. Convinced at last, Aubert founded an oratory. The oratory was expanded into a great abbey over time.

The origins of St Michael's Mount are traced to 495, when fishermen saw Michael standing on a ledge of rock atop a small mount off the coast near Penzance. St Michael's Mount, as it became known, was already an important trading market and port. It took on new significance with its association with Michael, and became a hallowed place. A Benedictine monastery was built on the rock in 1135.

Numerous other abbeys, monasteries and churches have been dedicated to Michael as well.

Raphael

Raphael, 'the medicine of God' or 'the shining one who heals', reigns as the primary angel of healing. He is often associated with the symbol of healing and medicine, the caduceus, a serpent or two serpents entwined around a staff. He oversees the physical well-being of the earth and its human inhabitants.

Raphael is not mentioned by name in the Old Testament, nor in the Protestant New Testament. His chief appearance is in the Book of Tobit, which is part of the Catholic canon. In that text, Raphael takes on the guise of a man to teach the arts of both healing and exorcism, and to urge people to a righteous life. He acts as a guide and companion on a journey undertaken by the young man Tobias, son of Tobit, thus making himself the angel of travel and safety.

Raphael has numerous titles and duties. He is counted among the seven anonymous angels who stand before God mentioned in Revelation, and is part of four orders of angels: seraphim, cherubim, dominions and powers. He is the angel of the evening winds, guardian of the Tree of Life in Paradise, and the angel of joy, light and love. He is sometimes identified as an aspect of the angel of great counsel; the angel of peace; the angel of prayer; the angel of repentance; an angel of the earth; and an angel of the planets.

Uriel

Uriel is the least familiar of the 'big four', but nonetheless wields great power in the angelic realm. One of the most important angels, he is described variously as an archangel, a seraph and a cherub. The name Uriel probably means 'fire of God' or 'God is my light.' Uriel's name does not appear in the Bible, but he plays prominent roles in non-canonical texts such as the Book of Enoch, where he is a heavenly guide and the angel who 'watches over thunder and terror'. In his role as a cherub, Uriel guards the Gate of Eden with a fiery sword in his hand. As a seraph he guards the flame of Truth. He also thwarts the demon Error, who leads men astray. He is one of the seven planetary rulers.

Uriel is usually portrayed as a stern angel. Enoch said he is head of the seven archangels, and presides over Tartarus, or Hell, where he pursues the punishment of sinners. According to the Apocalypse of St Peter, this punishment consists of burning sinners in everlasting fire, and hanging blasphemers by their tongues over unquenchable fires. On

Judgement Day, Uriel will break the brazen gates of Hades and assemble all the souls before the Judgement Seat.

Meditations for Working with the Angels of the Quarters

As the Angels of the Quarters, Gabriel, Michael, Raphael and Uriel create and organize a foundation and space for us. The square is a spiritual symbol of firmness, foundation and orientation. We can call on the angels as a group to obtain help and to assist us in our spiritual work.

Try these three exercises: The Spiritual Compass, Seasonal Signals, and Answers in the Elements.

THE SPIRITUAL COMPASS

The four angels each anchor a point on our spiritual compass:

1 Gabriel represents the east, which symbolizes the dawning of new awareness or new circumstances, a fresh start, and new opportunities.
2 Michael represents the south, which symbolizes things coming into fullness and fruition, abundance, action and activity.
3 Raphael represents the west, which symbolizes healing, releasing, and letting go of things that no longer serve our purpose.

4 Uriel represents the north, which symbolizes discipline, mental effort and planning.

The Spiritual Compass keeps us pointed in the right direction. In any given situation, the needle on the compass will point to what we need the most in order to stay on track. You can consult the Spiritual Compass for help in solving a problem, or simply on a daily or weekly basis as part of your life's navigation.

Before starting your meditation, prepare a clear question that you would like answered. In meditation, invite your guardian angel to participate. Visualize a compass and place each of the Angels of the Quarters at their appropriate stations. You can make a drawing to help you visualize this. In your mind's eye, see the needle of the compass moving freely around the dial. Ask your question and then allow the needle to point to the direction, or quarter, where you need to work in order to move forward. Accept where the needle goes without reservation or judgement. It will spontaneously move to the right place.

Once you have a direction, then address the angel who governs it. Ask for more specific guidance and help. You may be under the aegis of that angel for a period time, as circumstances are played out on the earthly plane.

If Your Needle Points East

Gabriel says that something new is coming. You may need to have patience and allow it to rise fully over the horizon like the day's new sun. Or you may need to open your eyes to the landscape in front of you to see the opportunities that are being presented to you.

If Your Needle Points South

Michael says that the time is right to take charge and take action. Make decisions with confidence. Or perhaps you are already on course, so persevere.

If Your Needle Points West

Raphael says that something needs to be released or healed first before other things can fall into place. Perhaps it concerns feelings and attitudes, or past wounds. Perhaps you have rifts in your present relationships that require your attention.

If Your Needle Points North

Uriel says that you need to do more planning and organization. Look inside – there may be inner 'house-cleaning' that needs to be done. Examine what needs to be organized in the outer world. Perhaps you need more self-discipline. Goals are not accomplished by wishing them so.

Sometimes the compass needle will fall between absolute directions. For example, if it points northwest, then consult both Raphael for releasement and Uriel for organization.

If the needle on the compass does not remain fixed, but continues to move around the dial, it indicates that you are not ready to ask the question, or you have doubts – or fears – about the process or answer, which are interfering in the process. When you have resolved these matters, ask again.

You can call on the Spiritual Compass at any time, and for any matter. You can quickly consult it on a mental screen within your mind's eye.

SEASONAL SIGNS

Another way to work with the Angels of the Quarters is with their seasonal symbolic associations:

1 Gabriel is spring, which represents beginnings, fertilization, new growth and freshness.
2 Michael is summer, which represents lushness and fullness.
3 Raphael is autumn, which represents the harvest, storage and saving.
4 Uriel is winter, which represents conservation, rest and contemplation.

For meditation work, start with a clear question. In meditation ask for the season that is the answer. Allow the response to rise up spontaneously within you without hesitation or judgement.

If the Answer Is Spring
Gabriel says it is time to plant one of those ideas you've had, but have put off due to other distractions. Plants cannot flower unless their seeds are earthed and nourished.

If the Answer Is Summer

Michael says it is time to tend to the garden you have already grown. Pull out the weeds and get rid of the pests. Make sure you give your garden plenty of spiritual nourishment and attention. Enjoy what you have created.

If the Answer Is Autumn

Raphael says it is time to reap your harvest. If you wait too long, it loses its value. Take what you have gained from your experiences and store them as wisdom. Accumulate your resources of time, energy, health and wealth.

If the Answer Is Winter

Uriel says it is time to take stock of the past and contemplate what you need to do next. Take time out for rest and contemplation. Examine your resources, and plan your next moves.

You can also use the seasons as time-tables for planning. For example, if you would like guidance on the best time to undertake a certain activity, ask for the answer in the form of a season. Once you have a general time-frame, you can ask for more specific guidance from the angel who governs that season.

ANSWERS IN THE ELEMENTS

The Angels of the Quarters are aligned with the four elements of air, earth, water and fire, each of which has symbolic meanings that provide insights for guidance. In meditation, ask your question, and then ask for the answer in an element. As in the other exercises, allow the answer to rise spontaneously within you.

The associations are:

1 Gabriel is air, which is communication and thought.
2 Michael is fire, which is energy and action.
3 Raphael is water, which is emotion and intuition.
4 Uriel is earth, which is physical resources.

If the Answer Is Air

Gabriel advises you to pay attention to communication. Perhaps you need to strengthen or repair communication, or establish new communication. There may be something that requires diplomacy or negotiation, or getting something in writing. Perhaps you need to be more mindful of your words. Or do you need to speak up about something that is bothering you?

If the Answer Is Fire

Michael advises you to marshal your energy carefully. Fire energy is busy and gets things done. It provides a take-charge, can-do leadership. When not managed well, fire goes out of control and destroys. The proper use of fire requires discernment: knowing when to stoke the flames and when to damp them down. Sometimes fire is necessary for purification, to get rid of 'dead wood' so that new growth can sprout in the ashes.

If the Answer Is Water

Raphael advises you to examine your emotions, and to look deep within to your true feelings that lie below the surface. Perhaps you need to be truthful about how you really feel. Pretending in order to please others serves no useful purpose in the long run. Perhaps you need to pay more attention to your intuition. Are you getting a calling to go in a certain direction, but are afraid to heed the call?

If the Answer Is Earth

Uriel advises you to check your impulses and weigh options carefully in a balance of logic and intuition. Pay more attention to energy, time, health and wealth – the resources of the physical plane. Don't let unproductive people and projects drain you. Invest yourself wisely. Perhaps you need to take a rest or time out. Or, perhaps it's time for you to get 'unearthed' – to come out of rest, inactivity and indecision and get back in the flow of life.

The Ladder of Angels

Just as human beings are organized into peoples, races, nations and communities on earth, angels are organized in the heavens and divided into orders, each of which has its own characteristics and responsibilities. The orders emanate from the Godhead. Those closest to God are concerned almost exclusively with the highest of spiritual vibrations, while those closest to earth are more involved in human affairs.

There is no general agreement on a single system of organization, either in Judaism or Christianity. The Bible gives the names of nine groups – angels, archangels, principalities, powers, dominations (or dominions), virtues, thrones, cherubim and seraphim – but does not specify their respective rankings or their celestial duties. Those details have been filled in by theologians, philosophers and artists.

The Kabbalah features ten orders of angels that correspond to the ten *sephirot*, or stations, on the Tree of Life.

In Christianity, the early fathers of the church discussed and organized angels into seven, nine, ten and eleven orders. The system that emerged as the dominant one to survive down through the centuries was a nine-level hierarchy developed by Pseudo-Dionysius, also known as Dionysius the Areopagite. According to lore, Pseudo-Dionysius was a man converted to Christianity by St Paul in Athens. More likely, he was an anonymous Christian Platonist and Gnostic writer who lived in the 5th or 6th century CE.

Pseudo-Dionysius said that the hierarchy of angels is a holy order that aims to achieve the greatest possible union with God. Probably the chief reason why Pseudo-Dionysius' celestial hierarchy rose to dominance was its adoption in the 13th century by St Thomas Aquinas, one of the most influential theologians of the church.

In the Pseudo-Dionysian scheme, the hierarchy of angels consists of nine orders divided into three tiers:

Tier I (closest to Earth)
1 – Angels
2 – Archangels
3 – Principalities

Tier II (middle)
4 – Powers
5 – Virtues
6 – Dominations

Tier III (closest to God)
7 – Thrones
8 – Cherubim
9 – Seraphim

The higher tiers possess all of the wisdom, abilities and illumination of the lower tiers, which in turn depend upon the immediate higher tiers, or choirs, for dispensation of the light and love of God. In the highest tier, the seraphim, cherubim and thrones receive illumination directly from God and send it down to the second tier of virtues, dominations and powers, who are concerned with heavenly order, the ruling of other angels, and miracles. The second tier in turn sends down illumination to the lowest tier of principalities, archangels and angels, who are concerned with the affairs of humanity.

Most human interaction with the kingdom of angels concerns the bottom tier. It may seem odd that the beings we consider to be so mighty and awesome are actually at the lowest and most dense level of the Ladder of Angels. This is appropriate and fitting, however, for they are best suited for the consciousness of everyday life. Angelic energy becomes more refined, subtle and powerful at every level up. However, the higher orders do make their illumination available to us, which we can access through prayer and meditation. The higher levels send down their energy, and it is transmuted by the lower orders into illumination that we can perceive.

The number nine symbolizes wisdom and completion. God is the centre and is both the Source of All Things and the return to the Source. From God emanates Oneness. Think of the angels as weavers, taking different strands of God's unconditional love and weaving it through Oneness, so that all Creation is held together in perfection.

The Ladder of Angels

The easiest way to understand the celestial hierarchy and work with its orders of angels is to envision it as a heavenly ladder that connects the human soul to God. We learn of this ladder in the first Book of the Bible, Genesis, in the story of Jacob, son of Isaac and grandson of Abraham. Jacob steals the birthright of his twin brother, Esau, and flees to his uncle with Esau in pursuit. On his way, Jacob stops for the night, taking a stone as his pillow. He dreams: 'a ladder was there, standing on the ground with its top reaching to heaven; and there were angels of God going up it and coming down' (Genesis 10:12). God explains Jacob's high spiritual destiny: this land will be the dwelling of his innumerable descendants, and God will never desert him: 'I will not leave you until I have done all that I promised you' (Genesis 28:15). When he wakes up Jacob calls the place Bethel, meaning the 'gate of heaven'. He anoints the stone pillow with oil and sets it up as a monument, with which he promises faithfulness and to give a tenth of his wealth to God in return for his preservation and safe return to his father.

Perhaps Jacob did not realize it, but the dream was a gift of a great spiritual tool. The Ladder of Angels serves as a guide for us in our spiritual work. We can equate the rungs of the ladder with the different orders of angels. In our spiritual work we rise up the ladder in the ascent of our soul to God. At each level, the angels there assist us with specific tasks.

Jesus made a reference to the Ladder of Angels. In John 1:51, he says to his disciples, 'I tell you most solemnly, you will see heaven laid open and, above the Son of Man, the angels of God ascending and descending.' Thus, we are in constant contact and interaction with the heavenly host. The Ladder is always active.

The Ladder of Angels can direct us to the angels whose specific tasks meet our specific needs. In addition to asking your guardian angel for assistance, you can also ask the angels of the orders for help.

The following are descriptions of the organization of the Ladder of Angels. Each order is involved in certain activities, and each has a Contact Angel who is one of the leaders of the order. If you wish the help of an order, you can appeal to the Contact Angel or to the order as a whole. The response to your request may involve one of the members of the order, a group of angels, or the energy of the collective order itself. Some of the angel names will be familiar to you; angels, like us, are multi-tasking beings. The numbers assigned to the orders and tiers start with those closest to earth.

Tier I: The Realm of Human Nature

The first tier of the Ladder of Angels consists of the angels, archangels and principalities. These are the angels assigned to work closely with the affairs of the earth and human souls. They assist us in daily life, helping us to develop and refine our human nature and inner self into more godly qualities. They are our divine messengers of prayer and God's guidance.

ANGELS

Contact Angel: Gabriel

Angels open us to awareness of the angelic kingdom. Our guardian angels are in this level. Everything pertaining to the affairs of daily life are overseen by angels. If we pay attention to the guidance they provide, we develop our intuitive powers, our sense of our Higher Self – our connection to the Divine – and a vision of the spiritual path before us. Angels help us to make decisions that are in our highest good and the highest good of all. They help our piety, our ability to pray, and our faith. They fight against spiritual apathy. Through angels, our desire to lead better, more spiritual lives begins to bloom.

Gabriel, 'the hero of God' whom we met earlier, serves as the primary contact to the angel order. Gabriel announces new things coming into being. When we awaken to angels, they herald the dawning of a new spiritual consciousness within us. We receive revelation and spiritual instruction.

Call on angels to receive and manifest:

• Guidance
• Assistance with prayer
• Devotion
• Faith

- Happy personal relationships
- Solutions to personal problems

Call on angels to release and heal:

- Apathy
- Uncertainty
- Attachments
- Disharmony with others

ARCHANGELS

Contact Angel: Michael

The name 'archangels' comes from the Greek term *arch-angelos*, meaning 'chief messengers' or 'eminent messengers'. Archangels, also known as 'Holy Ones', are liaisons between God and mortals; they are in charge of heaven's armies in the battle against hell; and they are the supervisors of our guardian angels. They have a special place before God.

The order of archangels is concerned with spiritualized empowerment. Once we are awakened, we are called to bring forth spiritual works in the world. We declare ourselves boldly as travellers on the path of Light.

Archangels work to eliminate ignorance and darkness. As our spiritual vision broadens, we acquire wisdom about sowing well in order to reap a right and abundant harvest. We make better decisions from a higher spiritual perspective.

Michael, 'who is like God', is the contact angel of the order of archangels. Michael takes bold action to ensure well-being. He vanquishes the obstructions to our spiritual birthright of abundance and happiness.

Call on archangels to receive and manifest:

- Spiritual vision
- Wisdom
- Assertiveness
- Abundance
- Joy and happiness

Call on archangels to release and heal:

- Ignorance
- Idleness and laziness
- Inaction
- Anything that no longer serves a purpose for you

PRINCIPALITIES

Contact Angel: Haniel

Principalities, or 'princely powers', watch over the actions of the Earth's nations and cities – the visible world of humankind. Every nation has its own principality. They also govern and protect religion on this planet. Principalities can help humans call upon secret powers to establish their own authority. However, authority must be in balance with peace and harmony.

The ability to rule requires an ability to establish good order. A good ruler is firm but also merciful, and intuitively knows when to be one or the other. Rulers must demonstrate courage as an example to others. They know the importance of forgiveness. Principalities help individuals to develop all of these qualities and abilities.

The name of the principalities' contact angel, Haniel, means 'glory of God' or 'he who sees God'. Haniel rules all innocents and is an angel of benevolence, grace, love and beauty.

Call on the principalities to receive and manifest:

- Courage
- Mercy
- Benevolence
- Intuition
- Solutions to community and global problems
- Forgiveness
- Peace
- Harmonious group relationships

Call on the principalities to release and heal:

- Cowardice
- Disorder
- Disharmony among groups
- Conflict
- Disorganization

Tier II: The Realm of Effort

The second tier of powers, virtues and dominations is devoted to helping us with our actions in the world. Having refined our lower nature with the help of the first tier of angels, we feel a new call to help make the world a better place. Our concerns go out beyond the sphere of our own lives to the good of the collective.

POWERS

Contact Angel: Camael

Powers fight against evil spirits who seek to wreak havoc through human beings, and protect the divine plans initiated by higher angelic orders. They help us find strength to persevere and to stand up for what is right. When we need to reach deep within ourselves, powers come to our aid.

Powers also are concerned with salvation – not only ours, but the goodness of all things. They help us to open our hearts. They provide patience when we are tested by adversity. Sometimes we must find our true strength in forgiveness.

The name Camael means 'he who sees God'. Camael is a forceful angel who rules Mars and wages battles – just the kind of angel you want when life calls for strength and determination. He oversees divine justice, an important concept for us to understand. Divine justice addresses the highest good of all things, and works according to a cosmic timetable. Divine justice always prevails, but not necessarily in a time-frame of our choosing, or even in ways that we can see. When we surrender to divine justice, we must have faith that it will be delivered in the best time and manner.

Call on the powers to receive and manifest:

- Determination
- Inner strength
- Energy
- Decisiveness
- Wise use of power
- Patience
- Justice

Call on the powers to release and heal:

- Weakness
- Vengeful desires
- Aggression
- Selfishness
- Ego

VIRTUES

Contact Angel: Raphael

Virtues are 'the shining ones' or the 'brilliant ones'. The primary tasks of virtues are to execute miracles on earth and provide courage, grace and valour. Through virtues, God governs the seasons, elements and heavens. Humans receive power from virtues that strengthens them and enables them to fight constantly the enemies of Truth.

While all angels assist us in living according to virtues, this guidance especially comes from the virtues themselves, who embody and convey godly qualities as a model for humans to follow. Whenever we seek to do what is right, just, fair, moral and ethical, the virtues pay close attention. They assist us in eliminating patterns of thought and behaviour that interfere with the virtuous life.

Raphael, 'the medicine of God', lights the path of spiritual travellers. He is our guide on our soul journey, helping us to walk it with grace and beauty. He heals our blindness and shortsightedness.

Call on virtues to receive and manifest:

- Righteousness
- Strength of will
- Thanksgiving
- Grace
- Valour
- Miracles

Call on virtues to release and heal:

- Arrogance
- Envy
- Resentment
- Ingratitude
- Temptation

DOMINATIONS

Contact Angel: Zadkiel

Dominations regulate the duties of other angels and make known the commands of God. The term 'domination' refers to 'lordship', 'rule' or 'special meaning'. Another name for them is 'authorities', which also conveys their primary purposes. Dominations are concerned with the establishment of order and rationalism, which requires the ability to take command with majesty, but not in a self-serving, egotistical way. They help people fight wars and overcome their enemies in righteous causes, but they also are channels of mercy.

Zadkiel, the Contact Angel of the dominations, is also one of the nine rulers of heaven, and one of the seven archangels who stand in the presence of God. The name Zadkiel means 'righteousness of God'. Zadkiel is said to be the angel sent by God to stop Abraham from slaying his son Isaac. He is the angel of benevolence, and one of the angels of mercy and of memory.

Call on dominations to receive and manifest:

- Leadership
- Confidence
- Self-confidence
- Healing
- Hope
- Mercy
- Clarity

Call on dominations to release and heal:

- Passivity
- Doubt
- Futility
- Pessimism
- Hopelessness
- Confusion

Tier III: The Realm of Grace

THRONES

Contact Angel: Raziel

The term 'throne' refers to a symbol of majesty and the seat of God and God's glory. The angels who bear the throne are called thrones or chariots of God, and they work under the 'driving' or direction of the cherubim, the next order higher on the Ladder. Thrones are described as flashing wheels, the rims of which are ringed with eyes that see everything everywhere.

Thrones are characterized by peace and submission – they receive the fullness of God. They chant glorias to God and remain forever in his presence. They mete out a high level of divine justice, which operates on a large scale in the human world. They maintain the cosmic harmony of all universal laws. Through thrones humanity is knit together and collected into itself.

Thrones reside on a plane of heaven where material form begins to take shape – that is, where ideas and thoughts begin the process of manifestation. Thus, they govern the headwaters of creativity and inspiration.

Raziel, the Contact Angel for the thrones, is the angel of the secret regions of heaven and chief of the Supreme Mysteries, who is charged with guarding the secrets of the universe. The name Raziel means 'secret of God' or 'angel of mysteries'.

Raziel is the keeper of The Book of the Angel Raziel, the first book ever written in heaven. The Book of the Angel Raziel is made of sapphire, and contains all the secrets of the cosmos, including the mysteries of creation and even things that other angels do not know. When God expelled Adam from Paradise, he took pity on him and instructed Raziel to give Adam the book so that he could gaze into the mirror of all existence and see the face of God, and himself as an image of God. The book was passed down through the patriarchs. Noah consulted it for making the ark. King Solomon was shown the book by Raziel in a dream, and used it for learning his great magical wisdom and power.

According to lore, other angels were jealous that humans should be given such great knowledge. There is even one story that the envious angels stole the book and cast it into the sea, but God had it retrieved and restored to humanity.

In the Middle Ages, versions of a Jewish mystical text called the *Sefer Raziel* (Book of Raziel) made their appearance, as well as other texts referring to the book. The text contains the names and duties of the angels, the organization of the cosmos, the keys to the alphabets of the angels, instructions for making talismans and amulets, and prayers and incantations for directing ministering angels and attaining mystical states of consciousness with angelic help. Some sources credit authorship to either Eleazar of Worms or Isaac the Blind. Eleazar of Worms, who lived from 1160-1237, may have authored at least part of it. Most likely, the text was compiled in the 13th century. It was so highly revered that mere possession of it was said to prevent fire. By the 19th century there were 25 editions of it, and it is still in use today.

Call on thrones to receive and manifest:

- Equality
- Fairness
- Divine justice
- Selflessness
- Open-mindedness
- Creativity
- Inspiration

Call on thrones to release and heal:

- Prejudice
- Narrow-mindedness
- Rashness of words
- Thoughtlessness
- Inconsiderateness

CHERUBIM

Contact Angel: Cherubiel

The meaning of the name 'cherub' (cherubim is the plural) is uncertain, but perhaps means either 'fullness of knowledge' or 'one who intercedes'. The cherubim are often described as having four wings.

Cherubim are important figures of power and fierceness, necessary attributes for their job of conveying God's Absolute Truth. Rays of illumination emanate from them, enlightening all the lower levels of angels and assisting humans in the contemplation of the divine. They are the voice of divine wisdom, possessing a deep insight into God's secrets. They emanate holiness through the universe in order to ensure the success of Truth. The force of their vibration drives out illusion, ignorance and deception. They stand before God and reverence his throne, keep his seals, and constantly sing songs of praise to him. They personify the winds, the force of nature that brings change and clears obstructions.

Cherubim are mentioned 91 times in the Hebrew Bible. They also are described in Revelation in the New Testament. The cherubim make their first appearance in the Bible in Genesis 3:22. God places them at the east entrance to the Garden of Eden, guarding it with flaming swords.

The cherubim have another supremely important function, guarding the Ark of the Covenant, a gilded wooden chest that bears the mercy seat of God, from which God speaks directly to Israel. Exodus 25:10-22 describes God's instructions to Moses for building the Ark, and for making images of cherubim from hammered gold:

> *The cherubim shall spread out their wings above, over-shadowing the mercy seat with their wings, their faces one to another; toward the mercy seat shall the faces of the cherubim be (Exodus 25:20).*

When King Solomon built the Temple of Jerusalem, he placed images of cherubim in the innermost sanctuary. 1 Kings 6:23-35 describes two gilded olivewood cherubim ten cubits high, with wing spans of five cubits. Their wing tips touched the walls on each side and each other in the middle. The inner wings formed the throne seat for God. Other carved and gilded figures of cherubim were placed elsewhere in the temple.

The Old Testament prophet Ezekiel had stunning mystical visions of cherubim. Ezekiel 1:4-28, describes cherubim as carriers of the throne of God, who appear as 'living creatures' having four wings and four faces – of a man, an ox, a lion and an eagle respectively. They stand on straight legs that end in calf's feet. They are like burnished bronze. They have beside them four wheels with spokes that seem like wheels within wheels and gleam like chrysolite. The creatures and wheels move in any direction simultaneously without turning, and with flashes of lightning and sounds of thunder. Over their heads is a firmament shining like crystal. Above that is a throne like sapphire bearing the likeness of a human form like gleaming bronze and enclosed by fire: this is the glory of the Lord, who speaks to Ezekiel. In another vision, cherubim precede Ezekiel as he is lifted up to the east gate of heaven.

Revelation 4:6-8 describes four 'living creatures' who are six-winged and are full of all-seeing eyes, and who sing constant praises to God.

The Contact Angel for the cherubim is Cherubiel, whose name is taken from the order.

Call on the cherubim to receive and manifest:

- Knowledge
- Spiritual wisdom
- Truth
- Enlightenment
- Discernment
- Revelation

Call on the cherubim to release and heal:

- Falsehood
- Deception
- Illusion
- Ignorance

SERAPHIM

Contact Angel: Uriel

The seraphim are the highest and closest angels to God, and are described as having an intense, fiery energy. The name seraphim may be derived from the Hebrew verb *saraf*, which means 'burn', 'incinerate' or 'destroy', and probably refers to the ability of seraphim to destroy by burning. According to the Book of Enoch, the seraphim are so-named because they burn the tablets of Satan. Every day Satan sits down with Sammael, prince of Rome, and Dubbiel, prince of Persia, to write down the sins of Israel on tablets. Satan gives the tablets to the seraphim to take to God so that God will destroy Israel. But the seraphim know that God does not wish to do so, and so they take the tablets and burn them.

Seraphim are described as having six wings which correspond to the six days of creation, and each wing is as big as the fullness of heaven. Each angel has 16 faces, four facing in each direction, and each face is like the rising sun, the light of which is so bright that even the other high-ranking angels, including the cherubim, cannot look upon it.

The prophet Isaiah had a vision (Isaiah 6:2-3) in which he saw God on his throne with six-winged seraphim standing above him. Two wings covered their faces and two their feet – probably to protect them from the intense brilliance of the Lord – and the other two wings were used for flying. The seraphim called out to each other, 'Holy, holy, holy is the Lord of hosts; and the whole earth is full of his glory.' One seraphim took a burning coal and touched it to Isaiah's lips, proclaiming that his guilt was taken away and his sin forgiven.

Seraphim are the created representations of divine love, the fire of which consumes them and keeps them close to the throne of God. They are the only angels to stand above the throne. They establish the vibration of love, which in turn creates the field of life. With their fiery energy, they purify everything and dispel the shadows of darkness. They help humans perfect the flame of love and charity, and overcome selfishness. Above all, they open our understanding of unconditional love, which is so pure and intense that it purifies whatever receives its grace.

Due to their high energy, seraphim are seldom directly perceived by human consciousness. However, when we call on them for assistance they, like the cherubim and other high angels, send their help to lower orders for transmutation so that it can be given to us.

Uriel, 'the fire of God', is the Contact Angel of the seraphim. He is charged with holding the vibrations of Truth and Unconditional Love, and seeing that they are dispersed throughout the universe. He is disciplined and dedicated to this task, and he moves swiftly to eradicate any shadows.

Call on the seraphim to receive and manifest:

- Charity
- Good-will
- Compassion
- Humanitarianism
- Unconditional love
- Comfort

Call on the seraphim to release and heal:

- Selfishness
- Hate

Working with the Ladder of Angels

The nine orders of angels co-ordinate with your own guardian angel in assisting you with your needs. If you make a request to your guardian angel, the angel consults with the best orders to get the job done. You can also petition the orders themselves; your guardian angel will automatically be involved.

You do not need to know the individual names of each and every angel who participates in actions on your behalf; many times, we are aided by a collective of angels. When asking for help, use the name of your guardian angel, the name of the Contact Angel of one of the orders, or the name of an order as the keys to open the door to heavenly help. Let the angelic realm organize the response that is best for you.

The more you work with the Ladder of Angels, the more you will develop a picture and understanding of the workings of creation and your participation in it.

The following are ways you can work with the Ladder. Undoubtedly you also will be inspired by your guardian angel to create your own work with this wonderful tool.

Climbing the Ladder

This meditation-and-action plan will help you develop flexibility in accessing different states of awareness, and will help you with self-improvement and the restoration and maintenance of well-being. You will move up and down the Ladder, ascending to expand your consciousness and descending to bring your new insights into your life.

You will work with each level on the Ladder for a specific period of time. I recommend a minimum of a week at each level. Set aside regular meditation time to contemplate the qualities of the order, and how you see them reflected in your own life. Select areas from both lists of receive/manifest and release/heal (as on pages 94–5), and ask the angels to help you discover how to accomplish these tasks in your life.

For example, you might begin with the first order of angels by contemplating what it means to be an 'angel' in life. An angel is called to a higher standard – how are you called to a higher standard? Perhaps you need to strengthen your faith, or heal a relationship. You may have attachments that are holding you back.

Moving up to the next level of archangels, you might contemplate what it means to you to be spiritually empowered, and how you feel called to heal ignorance and darkness. You might focus on ways to improve abundance in your life. Perhaps you've been lazy about getting on with plans. Seek to release the blockage and obtain guidance for moving ahead.

Every week, move up one rung of the Ladder, and repeat the process. Keep a record, and add to the lists of receive/manifest and release/heal as you get fresh ideas.

Organize your insights into an action plan that you can implement. Action on our part is necessary for the heavenly energies to take hold in the physical world. Your action plan doesn't have to involve major changes in life, though at times these may be necessary. Sometimes the smallest changes result in significant shifts. The spiritual path is travelled one step at a time. The important thing is to have a *feasible* plan.

You will experience more rapid progress if you can devote time every day to the Ladder. Even a few minutes will reap a fruitful harvest. My own preference is to make time at the start of the day, which raises the entire day to a higher plane and lifts my spirits. Experiment to find your ideal time.

Affirmations of Truth

Affirmations – positive statements – are a powerful way to work with the Ladder. Affirmations help us build positive states of consciousness that influence us for the better. When they take hold deep within us, they can help bring about significant change.

Every level of the Ladder has its own 'Affirmation of Truth', a declaration that embodies a specific state of consciousness or being. In this exercise, you move up the Ladder by devoting attention to each affirmation in your daily meditation and contemplation. The affirmations are described below.

Sit in a quiet space and make the affirmation. Imagine yourself as a vessel receiving the outpourings of the heavens. Ask to receive guidance that will illuminate the meaning of the affirmation to you.

General questions to consider are:

- How is this affirmation expressed in me?
- How does this affirmation relate to the angelic order?
- How can I better express this affirmation? In daily life? In my role as a cosmic citizen?

The affirmations for the orders are:

Angels	'I do'
Archangels	'I will'
Principalities	'I know'
Powers	'I love'
Virtues	'I create'
Dominations	'I see'
Thrones	'I become'
Cherubim	'I am wisdom'
Seraphim	'I am love'

ANGELS: 'I DO'

The order of angels helps us to make our way in the world. They – including your guardian angel – are the messengers of guidance concerning everything that affects us. Angels help us to act in a more responsible way – they open the first steps to spiritual awareness. In your meditation, review your current status in various areas and ask, 'What can I do to do better?'

ARCHANGELS: 'I WILL'

Once we open our consciousness to a more enlightened state, the universe asks us to make a pledge to follow the path of Light. Once we are awakened, there is no turning back. We must release what no longer serves us in order to move into a higher dimension in our relationship with the divine, and in our service. The affirmation 'I will' makes the commitment. As you affirm this, guidance is given for the next step.

PRINCIPALITIES: 'I KNOW'

The princely powers reveal to us how to act from a position of command and authority. This is made possible by the knowledge that comes from our experience in walking the path of Light. The knowing of the principalities comes to us in intuition – our sense of internal certainty as to what is good and what is not. The affirmation 'I know' reveals information and knowledge now available to you for certain purposes.

POWERS: 'I LOVE'

The powers are warriors and judges on the side of divine justice and right. When the forces of evil threaten harmony, they wage fierce battle as the army and police force of the universe. However, their ferocity is not driven by a lust for violence, but by love. Love establishes order, and when love is threatened, appropriate measures must be taken. Powers work to maintain divine order through love. They know that sometimes justice is needed to restore balance.

In contemplating the affirmation 'I love', examine how you have maintained balance in your own life. Have you allowed fear to take control? Do you assert your power in a dictatorial way? Are you fair or unfair? If there are areas of your life that are out of balance, ask how the power of love can help.

VIRTUES: 'I CREATE'

The virtues help us literally to embody virtues. By so doing, we create a new and better world. We express our true selves. We discover that when we are truly aligned to divine love, we are the channels of miracles.

The affirmation 'I create' opens a limitless horizon of possibilities. We can bring our greatest dreams into being. Perhaps you will receive guidance for bringing a cherished dream into manifestation. Perhaps you will be awakened to a dream that you did not yet know was within you, awaiting your recognition. Virtues help you manifest your greatness.

DOMINATIONS: 'I SEE'

The dominations see the big picture. They understand the weaving of destiny, karma and fate. They see the probable futures created by present circumstances, thoughts and decisions. When we have this insight, we can make better decisions. We can change our thoughts, beliefs and behaviour patterns. We become more mindful of the common good as well as our own personal interests. We take the common good into consideration, and we make the necessary sacrifices. We are generous in our forgiveness and mercy.

The affirmation 'I see' opens your eyes to a broader horizon. It also helps you to see things that are hidden. What do you need to see and understand?

THRONES: 'I BECOME'

Having worked and purified yourself in the lower and middle tiers of the angelic hierarchy, you are ready to move into a much higher state of awareness. You see yourself not just as a person, a human, or even a solitary soul with its own agenda. Rather, you see yourself as a participant in a glory you glimpse but cannot yet fully comprehend, and which draws you to its centre. You 'become'.

When you make the affirmation 'I become', the thrones help you to undergo shifts of awareness that at first seem quite subtle, but reveal themselves to be quite deep and profound. You cross a threshold of knowing in which light and love pour into you on higher frequencies.

CHERUBIM: 'I AM WISDOM'

The affirmation 'I am wisdom' reflects being born into a fullness of knowledge of Truth. This wisdom bypasses explanation in words – it simply becomes part of the fabric of the soul. We move from becoming to a state of being, to the 'I am'. From the deepest part of our being, we understand how we are conduits for God's grace to come into manifestation in the world. We participate in a wisdom and divine order that is of the earth, but transcends the earth. Wisdom shines a spotlight on ignorance and illusion. The cherubim give us help in removing those shadows.

In meditating on the affirmation 'I am wisdom', ask how you can bring God's wisdom into the world for the benefit of all.

SERAPHIM: 'I AM LOVE'

The seraphim are focused on love of and devotion to God. All of their essence is devoted to divine love. The emanations of their devotion stream out to the furthest reaches of the cosmos. The affirmation 'I am love' pulls us up to the highest possible vantage point. Look at all of the areas in your life. Some will be governed by love and others not. Where you find upset, unhappiness and tension, ask how you can be love. Bearing the essence of love may have surprising answers for you.

Affirmations of Truth can be augmented with the guided meditations provided in the next section. Keep a record of your insights. Devise action plans.

Jacob's Dream Ladder

This exercise takes its name from Jacob's empowering dream of the angels moving up and down a ladder between heaven and earth. Dreamwork with the Ladder of Angels opens new vistas to spiritual growth, in which your dreaming mind works while you are asleep. Jacob's Ladder requires some familiarity with dreamwork, as dreams speak in metaphors and symbols.

Follow the procedure outlined in Climbing the Ladder (pages 112–13), focusing on one level of the Ladder at a time, over a period of time. Identify the specific areas with which you would like angelic help. Prior to sleep, formulate a question asking for guidance. For example, your question might be, 'How can I improve my relationship with _____?' Spend some time meditating on the question, and ask the angels to deliver guidance to you while you sleep. In the morning, record whatever you remember of your dreams. When you have more time, interpret the dream for the answer to your question.

Sometimes the answer doesn't come specifically in a dream; nonetheless, the processing has been done by the dreaming mind. You may know the answer when you awaken, or you may suddenly realize the answer in a flash of inspiration later in the day.

If you have not done much dreamwork in the past, you can still do this exercise quite productively with the help of a good dream guide.

The All-Seeing Mirror

The outer world – our daily life and environment and the world at large – are reflections of our inner world. If we are full of uncertainty, pessimism, hate, distrust, anger and fear, we will project those states of consciousness out and make them our reality. If we are full of love, confidence, trust, faith and optimism, we create a much better and more desirable world, from the circle of our personal life to the global community of planet Earth. Daily life – and the affairs of the world – are only as good as what we bring into being through our thoughts, emotions and actions. We are never victims of 'others', only ourselves. If you watch the news and think the world is in a sorry state, be aware that you helped to create this condition! You created it in numerous ways, through your actions and your inaction. The enlightened soul does not despair by this awakening, however, but resolves to move forward in a higher and better way.

Use each level of the Ladder as a mirror that reflects back to you your performance in the virtues and qualities associated with that level. The reflections can help you see where you are in need of improvement, and can be used as a foundation for your prayer, meditation and spiritual action in the world.

Additional meditations for specific angelic help are provided in the next chapter.

The 22 Angels of Mastery of Life

This section introduces you to working with 22 angels who govern key areas of life and soul development. Each angel emanates from one of the nine orders of the Ladder of Angels, though the qualities they represent transcend boundaries in general.

For every angel, there is a note of the order from which that angel emanates, a discussion of the qualities and virtues that angel represents, and how that angel can help you with specific needs. The quality or attribute of the angel serves as its name, such as the Angel of Abundance.

A specific guided meditation is provided for each angel. Every meditation is self-contained, from beginning to end. Thus, you will be able to go straight to any angel and begin working immediately with that energy, without having to refer elsewhere. As with other guided meditations in this book, you can do them on your own as self-study, but you will find it rewarding to work with a partner who can read the meditation induction for you (or you can tape-record the meditation yourself). Soft music in the background will aid your experience. The ellipses (...) indicate pauses, which pace the meditation.

Your guardian angel is an automatic participant in these meditations, as well as in any endeavours you undertake. An invocation and a closing are provided for the guardian angel; you may add your guardian angel's name.

Whenever you are in difficulty or a state of indecision, consult one or several angels in these meditation guides. I also recommend that you take angelic meditation journeys as a regular part of your personal growth.

You will also benefit from these meditations simply by reading them. You will find them inspiring and evocative. Try reading them at night prior to sleep. Take note of your dreams and your insights upon awakening.

The angels are arranged alphabetically according to their area of governance.

The Angel of Abundance

Emanates from: Archangels

The metaphysical law of abundance tell us that the bountiful universe holds a supply of unlimited good for all souls. We can enjoy the prosperity of health, abundance and love. There is no need to suffer lack. When we are attuned to God, we see this great abundance, and we bring it into manifestation.

What is real prosperity? Too often, we equate prosperity with money piled up in the bank. True prosperity is living in accordance with divine love. When our hearts are filled with divine love, we set things right on the spiritual plane, which in turn sets things right on the material plane.

Through divine love, we banish fear. It is fear that breeds poverty and other ills. Fear creates a fertile ground for worries and negative thoughts to take hold, and thus generates the very conditions of lack that we seek to escape. Fear creates resentments, judgements, attachments and a 'debt mentality' that leaves us constantly checking the ledger-book of life.

When we forgive ourselves and others – when we love ourselves and others – when we have faith that our unlimited good can be obtained – we manifest true prosperity. We find the right job, the right home. We have enough money to take care of our needs. We have the family we desire. We are happy in our relationships, and we meet whatever tests and challenges come our way. Most important, we are close to God, and allow the living love of God to flow through us in all that we do and all that we bring into creation.

Prosperity-consciousness is established by eliminating negative thoughts concerning lack. This builds a positive atmosphere. We affirm our abundance, no matter what we have. Even if our wallet is empty, we deny this lack and affirm that we are filled with the bounty of God. Knowing that words have great power to set forces in motion, we allow no words of poverty to limit us.

In order for our affirmative prayer, positive thinking and right action in the world to take firm hold, they need to penetrate into the depths where the cellular consciousness resides, and where true change takes place. Part of us cannot doubt that abundance can be truly ours, rightfully ours, and that it surrounds us all the time.

What we think and believe, individually and collectively, becomes absorbed into the minds of our cells. We cannot truly evolve to our fullest potential until we learn to bring divine light into the cells. Then we free ourselves from limitation.

To manifest true abundance, we must first bring our consciousness into attunement with the Source. The Angel of Abundance stands ready to aid us. This attunement establishes a link for the energy to flow into us through our entire being of body, mind and spirit. In this attunement, we rest in the total conviction that all of our needs are taken care of in divine order. When this field of consciousness is established, we are guided and inspired according to our highest good. It then becomes easier to bring specific goals into manifestation. It's not uncommon for goals to change as we realize exactly what is our highest good, our true purpose. We learn what we really want, or need, rather than what we *think* we want.

Properly attuned, we can use affirmations and prayer in productive ways. Affirmations, in which we proclaim what we seek as already manifest, are declarations of Truth. Prayer is an act of Truth. Through prayer, we set in motion the forces that enable us to manifest the picture of our affirmation. Thus, when we are sick, we do not say we are sick, but affirm that we are healthy. When we are poor, we do not say we are poor, but affirm that we are abundantly rich. To claim our gifts from God, we use affirmations to expand our horizons without limit. Prosperity is ours when we keep ourselves centred on God.

MEDITATION

I centre myself in a comfortable position ... I focus attention on my breath, seeing it as light and energy which flows down from the Source through the crown of my head ... filling my body with radiance ... and flowing out through the soles of my feet ... so that I am connected to the inspiration of heaven and the grounding of the earth ... I then breathe in slowly three times ... one breath to relax more deeply and let thoughts and tension drain away ... one breath to centre my attention in stillness ... and one breath to expand my consciousness to the space around me.

I invoke with prayerful and loving intent my guardian angel and the presence of the Angel of Abundance, to share this journey with me ... assisting me with seeing things in new ways ... and inspiring me to take loving action in the world ... Now before me arise impressions of the Angel of Abundance ... I take a moment to observe ... and to give thanks for my partnership with the angelic realm.

From my still point within, I expand my consciousness out around me ... it goes further and further out into space ... staying firmly within me at all times ... My awareness extends into higher and higher planes ... I soar with the Angel of Abundance ... I am lifted in divine light and love ... I am in perfect peace.

I become aware that I am connected to the Source of All Being ... and that I am more than connected ... I am part of the Source ... I cannot be separated from it ... the I AM that is me is part of the cosmic, infinite, eternal I AM THAT I AM ... a limitless perfection of abundance ... love ... and wholeness ... I am part of this, too.

I ask the Angel of Abundance to show me my true abundance ... before me the Angel reveals the bounty and treasure that is mine ... I experience it in awe and glory ... I experience the abundance I have already known in my life ... and the abundance that lies waiting for me to manifest.

I ask the Angel of Abundance to show me the truth about abundance ... its meaning ... its essence.

I absorb the teachings deep into my being ... I imagine the teachings as light that penetrates my body ... and goes into my very cells ... bathing them and nourishing them with truth ... I understand abundance ... I accept abundance ... I manifest abundance ... I become abundance.

I ask the Angel of Abundance to show me how I can bring greater abundance into being ... into my life ... into the world ... into the service of Oneness through love ... The Angel has been waiting for me to ask ... and the answers flow readily to me in many ways ... I take my time to experience and absorb them all.

From this experience, I allow to come into my mind an affirmation ... my proclamation of abundance.

I take three measured breaths ... feeling the breath flow through my body ... reconnecting me to the present moment in time, space and place ... I give thanks to my guardian angel and the Angel of Abundance for the blessing of this experience ... and I return refreshed from my journey.

The Angel of Comfort

Emanates from: Seraphim

One of our greatest needs is to heal loss, grief and bereavement. The passing of a loved one, the end of a relationship and serious setbacks in our health and careers can seem like tidal waves threatening to engulf us in sorrow and despair. Loss creates a canyon of emptiness that we fear may never be filled again. The Angel of Comfort stands ready to take our burdens and bestow healing that can help us accept and let go, forgive, reconcile and resolve – and to restore our faith in the present and the future.

Prayer is our most powerful means of healing loss. The Angel of Comfort absorbs our tears and transmutes them into diamonds of light and renewal. It helps us to find our lifeline of strength, hope and peace. In grieving we acknowledge our loss, and honour what we have lost. It is important to grieve, and it is equally important to move on from grief. The Angel of Comfort helps us to see that we are not left with ashes, but with treasures – gifts of grace and spirit that make our lives more meaningful. Life will not be exactly the same, but life is ever-changing. In our healing from loss, we have an opportunity to raise life to a higher level.

Despite the healing connection fostered by prayer, praying may be the hardest thing to do. A staggering loss can make prayer seem ineffectual, and we may feel we have lost our ability to pray at all. This can make us feel guilty and disconnected from our faith, which compounds our inner turmoil. We must remember that the door to God is always open. We are never turned away, no matter how long we have been gone, or how hard and bitter we feel. If we but think of the Angel of Comfort, we will be immediately connected to divine compassion and comfort. Even if we can spend but a few minutes at a time in prayer, we will be given spiritual help beyond measure.

St Padre Pio, who was close to the angels, said, 'Your tears were collected by the angels and were placed in a gold chalice, and you will find them when you present yourself before God.'

MEDITATION

I centre myself in a comfortable position ... I focus attention on my breath, seeing it as light and energy which flows down from the Source through the crown of my head ... filling my body with radiance ... and flowing out through the soles of my feet ... so that I am connected to the inspiration of heaven and the grounding of the earth ... I then breathe in slowly three times ... one breath to relax more deeply and let thoughts and tension drain away ... one breath to centre my attention in stillness ... and one breath to expand my consciousness to the space around me.

I invoke with prayerful and loving intent my guardian angel and the presence of the Angel of Comfort, to share this journey with me ... assisting me with seeing things in new ways ... and inspiring me to take loving action in the world ... Now before me arise impressions of the Angel of Comfort ... I take a moment to observe ... and to give thanks for my partnership with the angelic realm.

I place myself in the loving hands of the Angel of Comfort ... and feel myself cradled in a warm and loving light ... The light moves into me ... soothing my entire being.

It is all I can do to make a simple prayer ... I feel over-whelmed in deep sorrow ... sometimes to the point where I think I cannot go forward another day ... and I feel so empty.

I release my sorrow and emptiness into the loving embrace of the Angel of Comfort ... The angel sends to me nourishing beams of divine love ... and I feel complete acceptance, just as I am.

I ask for my grief to reach a turning point ... and for the Angel of Comfort to help me take difficult steps ... I know I must do some forgiving ... and especially forgive myself for the shortcomings I have seen within me ... I realize that others around me do care deeply ... even though they are limited in their ability to help me.

I ask for help in accepting my loss ... And I ask for help in finding my way again ... May I see light ahead of me instead of darkness.

I ask for help to find meaning in what I have lost ... and what I can do to honour it ... I ask to feel gratitude for the gifts shared ... and the gifts left behind ... May I help others who are also in need.

I know that joy and pleasure are still mine ... and will return in fuller flower ... I know that I am meant to live a joy-filled life ... and to do so does not diminish what has passed away ... I live gladly and with purpose.

I know that whenever I am in need of comfort ... the Angel of Comfort will be at my side.

I take three measured breaths ... feeling the breath flow through my body ... reconnecting me to the present moment in time, space and place ... I give thanks to my guardian angel and the Angel of Comfort for the blessing of this experience ... and I return refreshed from my journey feeling great peace.

The Angel of Creativity

Emanates from: Thrones

Many artists speak of having a muse – a divine or higher source of inspiration and ideas that powers their imagination and creativity. That muse is the Angel of Creativity.

Creativity is not limited to the arts. Creativity is the vital juice of life itself. It is the energy, power and inspiration that we put into everything that we do. Creativity is not what we bring into being, but *how we live life*.

Each of us possesses powers to create meaning and

purpose in our lives. The Angel of Creativity shows us how to open up to the forces surrounding us – the life-giving powers, the powers of creation that exist in nature – and draw them to us, transforming ourselves into whatever we aspire to be.

Creativity gains from life experiences. It grows from our powers of observation of how things work in the world. The creative soul is acutely interested in learning the basic structure underlying all things, as well as the patterns, cycles and rhythms that exist in the world.

Creativity both fosters love and springs from love. If we love what we do and love life, our creativity is enhanced, which in turn increases our love and enthusiasm.

Creativity requires boldness and the ability to take risks and experiment. The creative soul knows there are no absolute failures. Lessons are valuable and produce knowledge that can be used again later.

The more we engage in a flow of creativity, the greater grows our self-confidence. We achieve the perfect balance between the rational and the intuitive. We are firmly grounded in the material plane, and yet we also move with ease in the realm of unseen forces where opportunities are born. We have confidence and faith in our works and ideas and our ways of living, even if others do not appreciate them.

Many visionaries are ridiculed by others who lack creativity. In the early 19th century, the American engineer and inventor Robert Fulton saw with his faith-filled eyes that a boat could be propelled by steam. Others laughed and called him a fool. But Fulton persevered with his vision, and created the steamboat. He made visible what he could see in the invisible realm of ideas. People laughed at Henry Ford when he produced the first automobile, and said it would never replace the horse. They scoffed at Christopher Latham-Sholes when he created the typewriter in 1868. Similarly, the photocopying machine and the telephone were mocked as ideas with no practical value. When DeWitt Wallace conceived of the idea for a digest-sized magazine that would give people the highlights of the current media, giants in the publishing industry turned him away and urged him to abandon the idea. Wallace set up a publishing business in his garage in 1922. People predicted he would go bankrupt. But the little magazine caught on, because Wallace had seen the need for it with his faith-filled vision. Today, *Reader's Digest* is an international publishing powerhouse.

Faith, confidence, vision and love bring creativity into flower. But once we have the vision, we must act on it.

One of the chief duties of the angels is to sing praises to God. Their reason for being is literally their song. Our creativity is like that, too. When we find our true song, the music we are called to make in life, we become divine instruments of praise to God. We participate fully in creation. We embrace life with great love and joy.

MEDITATION

I centre myself in a comfortable position ... I focus attention on my breath, seeing it as light and energy which
flows down from the Source through the crown of my
head ... filling my body with radiance ... and flowing out
through the soles of my feet ... so that I am connected
to the inspiration of heaven and the grounding of the
earth ... I then breathe in slowly three times ... one
breath to relax more deeply and let thoughts and tension drain away ... one breath to centre my attention in
stillness ... and one breath to expand my consciousness
to the space around me.

I invoke with prayerful and loving intent my guardian
angel and the presence of the Angel of Creativity, to
share this journey with me ... assisting me with seeing
things in new ways ... and inspiring me to take loving
action in the world ... Now before me arise impressions
of the Angel of Creativity ... I take a moment to observe
... and to give thanks for my partnership with the angelic realm.

I turn my thoughts to contemplate what creativity is ...
what creativity means ... I feel the energy of creativity ...
uplifting ... fast ... rushing ... joyous ... intense ... pleasurable

... satisfying ... I think of times and circumstances when I have experienced these emotions and energies.

The Angel of Creativity touches the diamond point at the centre of my brow ... and I feel a pleasant electricity come through me ... raising my vibration and awareness to a higher plane ... My eyes are opened to new realities ... I rise into the heavens ... and as I ascend I hear the celestial singing of angels in their devotion to God.

I feel my song within me ... the song that is my life ... and who I am as a soul ... I join the choirs of angels and raise my own voice in song ... I sing my Song of Creativity ... It issues forth in multitudes of colours and sounds ... and weaves itself into the tapestry of all Creation ... Wherever I look ... my song is strong and good.

I am filled with radiant energy ... that pours forth from my entire being ... I watch it flow forth from my hands ... which are symbols of bringing forth works into the world ... I am filled with ideas ... and the ways to manifest those ideas.

I ask the Angel of Creativity to assist me in manifesting my true artistry ... in artistic works ... in works of service and charity ... in the work that sustains my daily life ... and in my spiritual and inner work.

May my creativity help and heal others ... May my small-est acts be filled with creativity ... May my soul be a fertile field for rich ideas to take root and flower ... May my life be a field of abundant harvests.

I take three measured breaths ... feeling the breath flow through my body ... reconnecting me to the present moment in time, space and place ... I give thanks to my guardian angel and the Angel of Creativity for the blessing of this experience ... and I return refreshed from my journey.

The Angel of Enlightenment

Emanates from: Seraphim

Enlightenment is a state of being, the outcome of the process of spiritual growth, study, work and living. It can seem elusive – until one day we have an epiphany that tells us we have become more enlightened.

Enlightenment is a never-ending process; one doesn't achieve it like a diploma, or go there like a destination. Enlightenment is embodied in our outlook, our way of living, and our understanding of Truth. Like Truth, enlightenment must be experienced.

The Angel of Enlightenment serves at an altar of spiritual gold that lies within the heart. To understand this altar, we can look to the story of the Annunciation, and to the wise words of one of England's early saints, the Venerable Bede. Several months before the angel Gabriel appeared to Mary to announce the birth of Jesus, a priest named Zechariah went to the temple to perform his duties, which included burning incense for the public's prayers. Zechariah was married to Elizabeth, a descendent of Aaron. Both were elderly and childless.

In the temple were two altars. One was made of bronze and was for the burnt offerings of sacrifice. It was near the front doors of the temple. The other altar was covered with gold and was for the burning of incense. It was near the entrance to the Holy of Holies, the place symbolizing perfect grace.

As Zechariah burned the incense at the altar of gold, an angel appeared to him and stood at the right side. The startled priest was fearful at the meaning of this, but the angel, who introduced himself as Gabriel, told him not to be afraid. Rather, God had heard the prayers of Zechariah and Elizabeth, and they would soon have a son despite their age. They were to name him John.

The vision and the news so affected Zechariah that he had difficulty performing his priestly duties. When he finally emerged from the temple, he could not even speak to the people gathered outside for prayer.

John the Baptist was born. When he was grown, he lived in the wilderness, preached repentance, baptized people and prophesied the coming of the One who would baptize 'with the Holy Spirit and with fire'. It was his honour to baptize Jesus, at which the heavens opened and the Holy Spirit descended in the form of a dove, while the voice of God proclaimed, 'Thou art my beloved Son; with thee I am well pleased.' And so marked the beginning of the ministry of Jesus.

In his homily on the nativity of St John the Baptist told in the Gospel of Luke, St Bede the Venerable points out the symbolic significance of the Annunciation experienced by Zechariah. Gabriel appeared on the right side of the altar of gold 'to point out that he was not promising humankind earthly and lowly things, but the joys of heavenly and everlasting happiness (which are commonly indicated by the right hand),' writes Bede. Gabriel promised these things 'especially to those who through their purity of heart can themselves become an altar of gold, those who are able to abide with attentive thought near the entrance of the heavenly kingdom, who are able to burn the sweet fragrances of their prayers with the fire of their love for God, [and] who can say with the prophet, *Let my prayer be directed like incense in your sight.*'

What a magnificent thought! We can make ourselves into altars of gold through devoted prayer and love of God. In so doing, we offer ourselves as crucibles of transformation, for love to permeate like the fragrance of incense into everything we do in life. The gold here does not symbolize earthly riches, but the spiritual treasures that come only through devotion and enlightenment.

In your daily prayer and meditation, visualize yourself as an altar of gold at the entrance to the kingdom of God. Affirm, *My heart is an altar of gold*. In this way you will make a place for the expansion of Light, Truth and Love within you.

MEDITATION

I centre myself in a comfortable position ... I focus attention on my breath, seeing it as light and energy which flows down from the Source through the crown of my head ... filling my body with radiance ... and flowing out through the soles of my feet ... so that I am connected to the inspiration of heaven and the grounding of the earth ... I then breathe in slowly three times ... one breath to relax more deeply and let thoughts and tension drain away ... one breath to centre my attention in stillness ... and one breath to expand my consciousness to the space around me.

I invoke with prayerful and loving intent my guardian angel and the presence of the Angel of Enlightenment, to share this journey with me ... assisting me with seeing things in new ways ... and inspiring me to take loving action in the world ... Now before me arise impressions of the Angel of Enlightenment ... I take a moment to observe ... and to give thanks for my partnership with the angelic realm.

My attention goes to my heart centre ... I focus my entire being within my heart ... which pulses in harmony with the heart of creation ... my heart is a vessel of love and unconditional love ... my heart is a chamber for prayer and devotion ... my physical heart sustains my body ... and my spiritual heart sustains my soul.

Within my heart is my altar of gold ... my heart is an altar of gold ... attended by the Angel of Enlightenment ... who assists in the transformation of experience and devotion ... into love and wisdom ... I light the candles upon the altar ... and I light the incense ... and I close my eyes and pray ... my prayer is to know God ... a simple prayer ... that encompasses All That Is.

I see my prayer as sparkling light ascending to the heavens ... where it is carried by the Angel of Prayer to the presence of God ... the prayer takes me deeper and deeper into myself ... until I am in a space where there are no longer words ... and I simply AM ... and I expand into this space.

In this space of spacelessness ... I stand at the threshold of heaven with the Angel of Enlightenment beside me ... we pass through gates and gates upon gates ... past sun, moon and fields of stars ... past rejoicing heavenly hosts ... deep into the kingdom of heaven ... and into a golden chamber ... which contains an altar of gold ... This is the altar of gold that stands at the heart of creation ... the altar is inscribed with symbols ... which become imprinted upon my consciousness ... and which can be grasped and understood only through understanding and enlightenment.

I place my hands upon the altar ... and when I do, I feel currents of a mystical power surge through me ... the Angel of Enlightenment touches my brow ... and I am initiated into a higher awareness ... I am changed ... and I know that in my prayer and spiritual study ... I will feel changes in how I think ... how I speak ... and in my course of right living ... I notice now how my very being has changed.

As I acknowledge crossing a new threshold towards enlightenment ... the chamber begins to shift ... and the angel and I pass through layers of heaven ... to return to the chamber within my heart and the altar of gold that is there ... I see that this chamber has been changed as part of my initiation ... its energy ... and its presence ... have taken on a more spiritualized light ... I look at the altar ... and see it is now inscribed with the symbols which have become part of me ... and which will make their Truth known ... in the unfoldment of my spiritual path.

I take three measured breaths ... feeling the breath flow through my body ... reconnecting me to the present moment in time, space and place ... I give thanks to my guardian angel and the Angel of Enlightenment for the blessing of this experience ... and I return refreshed from my journey.

The Angel of Faith

Emanates from: Angels

What does it mean to have faith? To believe in something we can't see? To persevere despite odds and obstacles? To hang on when all seems lost?

Much is said about faith, yet little is understood about it. We tend to associate it with religion. That is a limited view, for faith operates in all aspects of life. Without it we would be adrift in uncertain seas. We need faith in order to manage our lives. We place our faith in certain laws of nature. We need faith in ourselves and in our abilities, talents and skills. We need faith in our personal relationships. There is not one aspect of life that does not require faith in order to function at its optimum. When tragedy strikes, when the world turns upside down, it is faith that sees us through.

In the Bible, Hebrews 11 defines faith as 'the assurance of things hoped for, the conviction of things not seen ... By faith we understand that the world was created by the word of God, so that what is seen was made out of things which do not appear.' Oftentimes we cannot see what we strive for, and we lose hope, when instead we should persevere. The goal, the reward, has not gone away, but is merely momentarily out of sight. If we stay to the path, it will reappear around the next bend.

Faith moves in the realm of the unseen. It cannot be measured or held. Faith connects the physical world with the spiritual world – the Mind of God. Through faith, we come to terms with one of the fundamental laws of the universe, that thought creates reality. What we think becomes manifest. What we believe comes to pass. We see the possible and know we can make it real, no matter what circumstances are in front of us. How well and how quickly these manifestations occur depend upon our faith. Jesus told us that through faith, even a tiny amount the size of a mustard seed, we can accomplish anything – we can do all of the great works that he did, and more. 'According to your faith, be it done to you,' he says in Matthew 9:29. No matter how dire our circumstances, faith enables us to create and transform anew. The greater our faith, the greater results we obtain, and the greater works we do. Humanity's great inventions, artistic creations and insights of mind and soul have all been birthed with the help of faith.

With faith, we know that life itself is an ongoing proof of the covenant of God. We know that we will be provided for. We know that every problem will find a solution. We know that we will succeed.

Jesus taught transformation of consciousness by word and by deed. He said that belief and faith are key factors. He performed numerous supernormal feats that were the products of his transformed consciousness: he was a superb healer; he manifested food; he changed water into wine; he raised the dead; he walked on water; he teleported his disciples; he was telepathic, and knew the thoughts of others; he controlled the elements; he was transfigured into a body of radiant light. All of these things that he did are also within our ability – if we but have faith. 'He who believes in me will also do the works that I do; and greater works than these will he do,' says Jesus in John 14:12.

Jesus referred to the spiritual eye as the lamp of the body. When the eye is sound – that is, when it perceives the unseen and understands the principle of faith – then the whole body is full of light. When our bodies are full of light, we are true channels for the divine power of God to flow through us, manifesting what the spiritual eye knows and sees through faith.

If we put our faith only in what we see, we cannot manifest all the good that is ours. If we say, 'I'll believe it when I see it,' we will always fall short of the mark. Rather, we must say, 'I believe, and therefore I see.'

To build faith, we must affirm our unity with God and then have faith in the power of that unity. When we place our faith first in God and not in material things and circumstances, then we tap into the power of miracles.

MEDITATION

I centre myself in a comfortable position ... I focus attention on my breath, seeing it as light and energy which flows down from the Source through the crown of my head ... filling my body with radiance ... and flowing out through the soles of my feet ... so that I am connected to the inspiration of heaven and the grounding of the earth ... I then breathe in slowly three times ... one breath to relax more deeply and let thoughts and tension drain away ... one breath to centre my attention in stillness ... and one breath to expand my consciousness to the space around me.

I invoke with prayerful and loving intent my guardian angel and the presence of the Angel of Faith, to share this journey with me ... assisting me with seeing things in new ways ... and inspiring me to take loving action in the world ... Now before me arise impressions of the Angel of Faith ... I take a moment to observe ... and to give thanks for my partnership with the angelic realm.

I know I am the living embodiment of God ... Bolstered by the spiritual fire of faith, I am empowered to reach my goals ... I have been born with the spiritual birthright of miracle-making abilities ... I feel the power of faith in me

... and flowing through me ... I take a few moments to contemplate this spiritual power ... what does faith look like? ... what does faith feel like? ... what does faith sound like? ... how do I perceive faith within me as a symbol?

I turn my thoughts to the past ... and think of something I have accomplished ... something I have become ... because I had faith ... because others had faith in me ... each triumph is a jewel on the string of jewels that is my soul life.

I turn my thoughts to the present ... and think of how I am demonstrating faith today ... and where I need to demonstrate faith.

I am filled with the radiance of transcendent love ... the light of my spiritual lamp shines on the path ahead, illuminating a universe of unlimited potential ... I go forward with ease and confidence on this path of light ... faith shall never leave me ... and through faith I am always connected to God ... and to the angelic realm.

I call upon the Angel of Faith to strengthen me ... I know I can triumph over any obstacle, any setback or any adversity ... divine help, presence ... and power are always with me ... through faith, I rise above the ordinary ... and become master of my life.

I take three measured breaths ... feeling the breath flow through my body ... reconnecting me to the present moment in time, space and place ... I give thanks to my guardian angel and the Angel of Faith for the blessing of this experience ... and I return refreshed from my journey.

The Angel of Forgiveness

Emanates from: Principalities

Sometimes our greatest pain comes not from illness or adversity, but from difficulties in our relationships with others, especially those whom we love. We may feel irreparably harmed by the actions of another, whether family, friend or stranger. Betrayals, hurts and acts of violence may seem unforgivable and linger with us for years. What's more, we may feel doubly aggrieved if the other party seems to suffer no consequences and moves on, leaving us behind with a hard bitterness in our heart.

Sometimes we are truly and deeply wronged. And sometimes we prefer to believe we are wronged, when in fact we share a good part of the blame for a situation gone awry. No matter who's to blame, resentments and grudges only hold us captive to a spiritual darkness. We cannot truly heal until we learn to forgive. In forgiving, we put ourselves in harmony with the Truth of Being, and all transgressions are eliminated. We are filled with the unconditional, healing love of God. Our forgiveness may not change the other person, but it does change us in profound ways. There is no limit to the healing power of forgiveness, as Jesus illustrated when he tells Peter to forgive 'seventy times seven' (Matthew 18:22).

When we forgive, a tremendous healing floods our body, mind and spirit. It matters not whether we are forgiving a fresh wound or an old hurt – the liberating effect of divine goodness is the same.

Forgiveness does not mean that we are soft or that we accept being victims. Forgiveness is not silent consent. Forgiveness enables us to put in motion more positive forces of Truth and strength. Forgiveness demonstrates spiritual strength. When we forgive, we can replace negative emotions with love.

We should not be concerned about obtaining immediate results from our forgiveness. We cannot control the responses of others. Instead, we must rest secure in our faith that the forces at work will create change as and when it is needed. We no longer think in terms of right and wrong, but in acting according to our highest good. In this way, we set an example that works in subtle ways to elicit the best from others.

We can make great progress towards wholeness and unity with God by learning to forgive. By coming to terms immediately with adverse thoughts and feelings, we release them before they have a chance to take hold in our consciousness.

When the harshness of others seems to crush you, send out love and forgiveness. The power not only blesses you but goes forth to redeem the adverse conditions in the other.

MEDITATION

I centre myself in a comfortable position ... I focus attention on my breath, seeing it as light and energy which flows down from the Source through the crown of my head ... filling my body with radiance ... and flowing out through the soles of my feet ... so that I am connected to the inspiration of heaven and the grounding of the earth ... I then breathe in slowly three times ... one breath to relax more deeply and let thoughts and tension drain away ... one breath to centre my attention in stillness ... and one breath to expand my consciousness to the space around me.

I invoke with prayerful and loving intent my guardian angel and the presence of the Angel of Forgiveness, to share this journey with me ... assisting me with seeing things in new ways ... and inspiring me to take loving action in the world ... Now before me arise impressions of the Angel of Forgiveness ... I take a moment to observe ... and to give thanks for my partnership with the angelic realm.

The Angel of Forgiveness directs my attention to my heart ... looking there, I see a black arrow piercing it ... the arrow is a symbol of a hurt or a wound that still affects me ... I know there are others, but today in this moment I have entered into sacred space to work on the one before me.

I bring to mind the circumstances that created this wound ... the things that were done ... the words that were spoken ... the feelings I had when I was first hurt ... the feelings I have now.

I think of the person whom I blame for this wound ... I think of the reasons why I have not released this hurt ... I see that I have been holding on to the thought that a wrong was done ... The Angel of Forgiveness tells me that this hurt has been presented to me now because I am ready to forgive it and release it.

I call to mind the other person ... a name and an image ... as if they stand before me now ... I tell them I forgive them now ... I release the chains of pain that have bound us together ... At the instant of my forgiveness, streams of light come forth and the Angel of Forgiveness winds them around and around the other person ... until they are covered as if in a cocoon of light ... when I breathe out, there is love carried on the breath, and it energizes the light ... a transformation is taking place.

The cocoon of light breaks open ... and from within flies out a butterfly ... it is the most beautiful butterfly I have ever seen ... I notice its shimmering colours ... Suddenly the image of the earth is before me ... and the butterfly circles the globe ... with streams of sparkling light flowing down from it to the planet ... The Angel of Forgiveness tells me that whenever we forgive, no matter how small a matter ... a butterfly of healing light is released into the world.

My entire being is flooded with the light from the butterfly ... and I am filled with profound gratitude ... I am grateful to experience this love within me ... I am grateful to see divine understanding in a new way ... I am grateful to be free of the pain of wounds ... I am grateful that my act of forgiveness has brought new light not only for me, but for others as well.

I take three measured breaths ... feeling the breath flow through my body ... reconnecting me to the present moment in time, space and place ... I give thanks to my guardian angel and the Angel of Forgiveness for the blessing of this experience ... and I return refreshed from my journey.

The Angel of Healing

Emanates from: Dominations

The majority of our prayers are requests for healing. Most often we ask for healing of the body, but also we ask for healing of mind and spirit – our emotions, our self-esteem, our self-confidence, our ability to dream dreams and make them reality. Our need to be healed supercedes all desires and all other needs, save for basic survival. So often in life, the heart aches with wounds that cannot be assuaged save for comfort from the Divine, and so we reach out in prayer.

While it is important in the healing process to acknowledge and honour our wounds, the healing process is not complete without a refocusing of our attention on spiritual upliftment. We must raise ourselves from the darkness of despair into the light of renewal. Healing cannot fully take place until we rise like a phoenix from the ashes of our sorrowing.

True healing must come first at the soul level. We awaken our soul, which unifies body, mind and spirit with the Mind of God, the highest possible state of unconditional love, joy and wholeness. Thus we can overcome anything, be healed of all afflictions.

Our spiritual birthright is one of wholeness. Our spiritual body is the perfect counterpart to our physical body. In healing, we must begin by rejoicing in the perfection of our pattern as a gift from God. We accept our perfection, and bring our mental attitudes into alignment with the divine law of health.

Sickness, whether of body, mind or spirit, does not exist in Truth. When we illumine our consciousness with Truth, it begins to work out our health problems for us. As we work in concert with the Mind of God, a great new power is added to our consciousness. The miracles of Jesus were performed according to universal laws that we can learn to use ourselves. Spiritual ideas move the mind, and the mind moves the body. Jesus merged his mind with the mind of the Father. His works, he said, were done through the Father abiding within him.

All thoughts radiate energy and set forces in motion. When thoughts are strong enough and radiated over time, they become real. When we lift our thoughts to merge with the mind of God, our thoughts radiate with the speed of spiritual light and bring to pass healing, health and wholeness.

Prayer brings us into alignment with the Mind of God so that healing energy can flow through us, either for ourselves or for others. We may experience that connection and flow, perhaps as a warm, loving presence or light, or a 'feeling' in the body of being healed. Time does not exist in the realm of spirit, and thus all prayers are answered immediately. If we understand this, and understand Truth, healing happens immediately as well.

Our understanding of Truth enables us to see truth about healing – healing does not always mean cure. Regardless of what happens in the outer world, we are always guided to perfect our expression of God. When we pray in the faith that there is a flawless pattern for wholeness within every person, we enable that pattern to be expressed. The highest good always manifests for us.

MEDITATION

I centre myself in a comfortable position ... I focus attention on my breath, seeing it as light and energy which flows down from the Source through the crown of my head ... filling my body with radiance ... and flowing out through the soles of my feet ... so that I am connected to the inspiration of heaven and the grounding of the earth ... I then breathe in slowly three times ... one breath to relax more deeply and let thoughts and tension drain away ... one breath to centre my attention in stillness ... and one breath to expand my consciousness to the space around me.

I invoke with prayerful and loving intent my guardian angel and the presence of the Angel of Healing, to share this journey with me ... assisting me with seeing things in new ways ... and inspiring me to take loving action in the world ... Now before me arise impressions of the Angel of Healing ... I take a moment to observe ... and to give thanks for my partnership with the angelic realm.

I rest in a space of perfect peace ... and allow the space to expand around me ... the space transforms ... and I find myself before a great temple of crystal ... I take some time to notice the details ... the shape of the temple ... the colours of the crystal ... the way the light interacts with the crystal ... I see a doorway ... and in the doorway is the Angel of Healing ... who beckons me to enter.

Inside the temple I look around me ... and observe what is inside ... and on the walls ... there are torches of fire on the walls ... illuminating the interior with a warm and mysterious light ... I feel welcome here ... I feel at total peace ... I feel light and buoyant.

I follow the Angel of Healing through a long hall ... lit by torches ... we move effortlessly along ... and come out into a large chamber ... with an arched roof ... like a cathedral ... and columns that gleam golden white ... In the centre of this chamber is a pool of water ... the water is clear and completely still ... it looks very inviting ... refreshing.

The Angel of Healing tells me that this is heaven's Pool of Healing ... accessible by journey of spirit and intent ... which is described in the Bible as the healing pool at Bethesda ... where legend had it that whenever an angel came down from heaven ... and stirred the waters in the pool ... whoever entered it would be healed ... Whatever

I wish to heal can be healed now ... when the waters are stirred and I enter them.

The Angel reaches down and energizes the water ... which ripples like liquid crystal ... I think now of what in my life needs healing ... allowing the thoughts to come spontaneously, knowing that they are right for this moment ... and I enter the pool ... upon which a wondrous experience unfolds.

When I am done in the waters ... I emerge from the pool ... and the Angel of Healing gives me a new garment to wear ... it is made of light and represents the perfection and wholeness of my spiritual birthright ... I put it on ... and take on a shining new being.

The temple dissolves and I stand in a field of light ... the light is alive and it pulses with power ... it is raising my vibration ... I am surrounded by light ... I glow with light ... light radiates from within me ... as part of my divine perfection.

Thoughts of divine perfection as part of God's plan to fill my mind ... I accept my God-given perfection ... and put aside my past mistakes. I fix my undivided attention upon the Creator of my inner pattern of perfection ... everything within me ... all of my mental attitudes ... the centres of my consciousness ... and my physical being ... are raised to the high place in the Divine Mind where I see as God sees.

I see that healing is a spiritual path ... a reconnecting to God ... a remembering of who I am on a soul level ... I ask the Angel of Healing to help me to see what is the healing that I was born for in this lifetime ... What have I come here to learn? ... I know that healing exists in all of the aspects of my life ... What needs to be changed to initiate the process of healing? ... I allow thoughts and impressions to rise spontaneously in answer ... I take time to reflect upon them.

I take three measured breaths ... feeling the breath flow through my body ... reconnecting me to the present moment in time, space and place ... I give thanks to my guardian angel and the Angel of Healing for the blessing of this experience ... and I return refreshed from my journey.

The Angel of Hope

Emanates from: Dominations

Hope is an aspect of strength that enables us to keep going in the face of adversity and prevents us from falling into the abyss of despair. Hope fuels our perseverance. Hope is forward-looking; it helps us to envision a positive outcome, a better future.

Sometimes hope is our only lifeline and salvation. When hope fails, other things are at risk of failing, too: will, determination, even our desire to hold on to life itself. When medical conditions are grave, patients may hear the words 'no hope' from their doctors. However well-intended, the removal of hope may be the one thing that prematurely closes the door on faith in miracles.

There is *never* no hope. We should never give up seeking divine help.

Hope is like a furnace. The Angel of Hope stokes the furnace with divine love. When we are in need of hope, we can through prayer warm and restore ourselves with the heat of God's love.

Hope also creates a space for something new. We *hope* for peace, *hope* for success, *hope* for a better world, *hope* for the right relationship, and so on. This is altruistic hope. The holding of the hope is only the beginning. For the process to be completed, hope must be followed by action. Hope helps us to conceive of the action that will realize the hope – but we must put forces in motion ourselves. Without action, our visions for something better become wallflowers in the dance of life. They are left on the sidelines, looking pretty for a time, but then fading when no attention is paid to them. The next time you find yourself saying, 'I hope that ...' ask if there is action for you to take to make the hope reality.

The Angel of Hope helps us to use the power of hope in constructive ways: one, as a source of sustenance when we are put to a test; and two, to became active participants in the creation of a more harmonious world.

MEDITATION

I centre myself in a comfortable position ... I focus attention on my breath, seeing it as light and energy which
flows down from the Source through the crown of my
head ... filling my body with radiance ... and flowing out
through the soles of my feet ... so that I am connected
to the inspiration of heaven and the grounding of the
earth ... I then breathe in slowly three times ... one
breath to relax more deeply and let thoughts and tension drain away ... one breath to centre my attention in
stillness ... and one breath to expand my consciousness
to the space around me.

I invoke with prayerful and loving intent my guardian
angel and the presence of the Angel of Hope, to share
this journey with me ... assisting me with seeing things in
new ways ... and inspiring me to take loving action in the
world ... Now before me arise impressions of the Angel
of Hope ... I take a moment to observe ... and to give
thanks for my partnership with the angelic realm.

I connect now to the essence of hope that is within me ...
and has been with me always ... I allow myself to experience it ... perhaps it is a fire ... or a shaft of steel ... or
a willow tree that bends easily in the wind without

breaking ... I feel the vibration of hope like a steady generator ... ever-ready to provide the currents I need whenever I face trials or obstacles ... setbacks or losses ... I know that hope is part of my strength ... hope is part of my faith ... faith that the universe is working out the highest good in every situation ... and that for whatever happens, I will have what I need within me to meet it ... the presence of the Angel of Hope towers beside me as a pillar of invincible strength.

Giving thanks for this power, I turn now to think of my hopes that are dreams ... goals ... ambitions ... visions ... what do I hope for in my own life? ... I allow answers to come easily to my attention ... I feel the energy of the hope ... I think of the actions I have taken to make those hopes reality ... and the actions that remain undone ... Perhaps I have hopes but do not know what course of action to take ... I ask the Angel of Hope to help me see actions that have been hidden from my awareness ... I take some time to absorb the lesson.

I turn now to my hopes for humanity ... and the world ... and all sentient beings ... and allow answers to rise up within me ... I feel the energy of those hopes ... I think of actions I have taken to help bring those hopes into being ... and actions that still must be taken ... I ask the Angel of Hope for inspiration ... to see ways in which I can energize the community of souls ... to foster higher consciousness ... and the peace and harmony established by love ... I ask, what can I do? ... and I make a commitment within myself to follow through.

I take three measured breaths ... feeling the breath flow through my body ... reconnecting me to the present moment in time, space and place ... I give thanks to my guardian angel and the Angel of Hope for the blessing of this experience ... and I return refreshed from my journey.

The Angel of Joy

Emanates from: Archangels

What is joy? Is it happiness? Freedom from want? Having things? We often mistake joy for lack of want. If we have everything we think we could possibly want, then surely we will be joyful.

Perhaps you have discovered that material things do not guarantee joy. Money does not guarantee joy, nor does health or a relationship. We cannot demand joy from others by loving them, sacrificing for them or doing favours for them. We cannot find joy in the escapes of pleasure, for those are artificial and temporary highs.

Joy is not something that happens on the outside and works its way in. Joy starts within, and then touches the outer world.

Joy is a spiritual quality, a state of being. It springs forth in a soul whose spiritual compass is orientated towards God. In one of his sermons, St John-Baptiste-Marie Vianney said, 'Do you want to be happy, my friends? Fix your eyes on heaven; it is there that your hearts will find that which will satisfy them completely.' St Thomas Aquinas put it another way in his great philosophical work, *Summa Theologica*: 'Happiness is another name for God.'

When we put our intent and will into walking the path of Truth and light, joy comes into our life and never leaves it. Even when we are embattled, we still can tap a reservoir of joy that sees the goodness and purpose in life. We are better able to cope with all our experiences, the positive and the negative.

Our spiritual study of Truth leads us to have 'peak experiences' which are sudden flashes of intense happiness and feelings of well-being, and perhaps an awareness of 'ultimate Truth' and the unity of all things. In a peak joy experience, we feel lucky or graced. We release creative energies. We reaffirm the worthiness of life.

The soul whose spiritual eyes are open sees true beauty and thus experiences joy everywhere. Perceiving the beauty that is all around us, we enter into the heavenly House of Joy and Happiness. Life itself becomes a supreme treasure, each moment of it to be savoured.

We can become disconnected from joy when we suffer setbacks, and when we fail to water the soul with frequent prayer and spiritual study. The Angel of Joy can help us reconnect. Aspire to be like an angel: full of love, devoted to

God's service, and celebrating creation. St Basil the Great said, 'Is there a greater happiness than to imitate on earth the choir of angels?'

There are many legends of saints who tapped barren ground with their staffs, and healing waters gushed forth. Joy is like that. No matter what the landscape of life, joy can be found beneath the surface and brought out into the world. All we need do is tap our inner ground with prayer and a request for divine help. The healing waters of divine love and joy surge up in a never-ending spring.

MEDITATION

I centre myself in a comfortable position ... I focus attention on my breath, seeing it as light and energy which flows down from the Source through the crown of my head ... filling my body with radiance ... and flowing out through the soles of my feet ... so that I am connected to the inspiration of heaven and the grounding of the earth ... I then breathe in slowly three times ... one breath to relax more deeply and let thoughts and tension drain away ... one breath to centre my attention in stillness ... and one breath to expand my consciousness to the space around me.

I invoke with prayerful and loving intent the presence of my guardian angel and the Angel of Joy, to share this journey with me ... assisting me with seeing things in new ways ... and inspiring me to take loving action in the world ... Now before me arise impressions of the Angel of Joy ... I take a moment to observe ... and to give thanks for my partnership with the angelic realm.

I ask for a picture of the landscape of my life ... and I consider how I would like my landscape to be fuller, lusher and more vibrant ... I think of times when I have felt full of joy and happiness.

The Angel of Joy touches the point between my brows ... the energy centre of my spiritual vision ... and I see a picture of how joy springs from my mental outlook ... and from my work in the world ... I see how I embody the work of heaven in even small things throughout the day ... a kind word ... a compassionate gesture.

I see how joy springs from my attention to life and creation ... as when I notice the way a plant blooms ... or how clouds decorate an azure sky ... I see how joy springs when I take nothing for granted ... and I rejoice daily at the wonder of being in the world.

I see how joy springs abundantly from thanskgiving and gratitude ... when I think of my blessings instead of my lacks.

I see that there is no place ... and there is no moment ... where joy does not exist.

The Angel of Joy passes a hand over my eyes ... and when I can see again it is with new eyes ... I see a different landscape ... same things in different ways.

Beneath the terrain of my life lies a reservoir of the waters of divine joy ... I look down at myself and see that I am transformed ... I wear a simple cloth robe ... and I carry a staff ... just like the saints of old ... With the Angel of Joy beside me, I raise the staff and strike the ground three times ... I see a crystal pool of water well up from within the earth ... It widens and deepens ... and begins to bubble and ripple ... as it becomes a spring ... Reaching down ... I cup the waters in my hand ... and drink from the spring ... The water is like liquid shimmering stars ... and I feel it go down into my belly ... and spread to all parts of my being ... I am lit from within by the radiant waters of joy.

I am in the moment ... I am supremely happy.

I take three measured breaths ... feeling the breath flow through my body ... reconnecting me to the present moment in time, space and place ... I give thanks to my guardian angel and the Angel of Joy for the blessing of this experience ... and I return refreshed from my journey.

The Angel of Justice

Emanates from: Powers

We usually think of justice as the redress of a wrong, but justice actually operates on a much higher cosmic plane. Justice concerns the maintenance of balance and harmony in all things. The universe strives towards perfect balance. Every choice has a consequence. We either help to maintain balance, or we create imbalance. When we tip the balance we pay a price. Balance must be restored. Sometimes it is easy to do so. Sometimes it is not. The Angel of Justice is impartial to how balance is restored.

When we are fair to ourselves and fair to others, we are rewarded with balance and harmony. When we are out of balance, in our lives, in our relationships, in our pursuits, we are doing an injustice to ourselves, our friends, family and associates. But because we are doing the injustice, we must set things right.

By placing too much emphasis on work we can damage our family relationships. By finding balance, we enjoy the fruits of both worlds.

By placing too much focus on the material side of our lives we can leave ourselves spiritually deficient. By making time for material and spiritual pursuits, we feel wholesome and see purpose in everything we do.

By being too self-centred, we live life alone. By finding time for others, we benefit from their companionship, their counsel, their friendship.

By pushing ourselves too hard, we can end up sick. By knowing where to draw the line, we perform to peak capacity in all pursuits.

The list goes on. The choice is always ours.

Life is give and take. We have to find that proper balance if we are to live life to its fullest. We must learn to compromise. We must learn to find where to draw the line between work and home, between the material and spiritual worlds, between drive and pleasure.

Justice comes into play when a grievous wrong has been committed. If we have been wronged, we demand justice. We want it swiftly and in equal measure to our suffering. If justice is not forthcoming to our desires, we feel bitter and angry – even doubly wronged.

We must recognize that justice is not always meted out to suit our desires, but it *is* meted out. The Angel of Justice has a much loftier perspective than we do, and knows how perfect balance will be restored. The cosmic workings are complex. Justice may be done in a time and place far removed from us. Justice may be done without our knowing it. We must trust that justice is *always* done, and we must accept that it is done in the manner that serves the cosmic whole. If we tamper with this process and try to force justice, we only perpetuate cycles of imbalance.

Justice also implies living in harmony with nature. Nature, herself, is perfectly balanced. But because we spend our lives outside of and distinct from nature, we tend to be oblivious to the balance of the natural order. We think that nature exists to serve us and we do not need to share. Again there is a price to pay. Fouled air and water. Animal species disappearing from the face of the earth. A world out of balance. A world in danger of disappearing. It's another price we pay because of the choices we make.

An appreciation for justice also is a measure of our personal development. The more we understand the principle of justice, the more we practise it in our daily lives, the more we grow, the more we share in rewards, the more fulfilled we are.

The more we as individuals believe in justice, the more it is practised by our society and the more humankind will evolve.

MEDITATION

I centre myself in a comfortable position ... I focus attention on my breath, seeing it as light and energy which flows down from the Source through the crown of my head ... filling my body with radiance ... and flowing out through the soles of my feet ... so that I am connected to the inspiration of heaven and the grounding of the earth ... I then breathe in slowly three times ... one breath to relax more deeply and let thoughts and tension drain away ... one breath to centre my attention in stillness ... and one breath to expand my consciousness to the space around me.

I invoke with prayerful and loving intent the presence of my guardian angel and the Angel of Justice, to share this journey with me ... assisting me with seeing things in new ways ... and inspiring me to take loving action in the world ... Now before me arise impressions of the Angel of Justice ... I take a moment to observe ... and to give thanks for my partnership with the angelic realm.

I surrender to the divine law of justice ... and know that it works in accordance to the highest good ... in the manner and timing that serve the highest good ... I think of how I have been wronged ... and I examine to the fullest depths my feelings ... I ask the Angel of Justice to help me release all of the darkness and negativity I harbour within me ... I breathe in green light ... and the green sends a healing balm deep into my being ... the darkness and hardened emotions dissolve ... and depart from me ... borne away by ministering angels into the divine light of unconditional love ... the green light within me fills all spaces ... and I am filled with love ... forgiveness ... and understanding ... I give thanks for Justice ... and I know that it will be administered in accordance with divine will.

I ask the Angel of Justice to show me how to achieve better balance in life ... I take some time now to examine the areas shown to me ... and I give thanks for the solutions that are made known to me through my Higher Self. I make a pledge to strive for balance and fairness ... and I ask for the Angel of Justice to help me to stay on course.

I am mindful of the need for me to be in balance with nature ... I am respectful of the forces of nature and the sentient beings who reside in nature ... I resolve to be more careful in my treatment of nature ... and to act where possible to raise the awareness of others.

I take three measured breaths ... feeling the breath flow through my body ... reconnecting me to the present moment in time, space and place ... I give thanks to my guardian angel and the Angel of Justice for the blessing of this experience ... and I return refreshed from my journey.

The Angel of Love

Emanates from: Seraphim

Loving means many things. Acceptance. Nurturing. Support. Tolerance. Patience. Compassion. Healing. Forgiveness. As we move through life, and as we progress along the spiritual path of Truth, we awaken to the tremendous redemptive power of love. Love binds all things in creation together. Love emanates from the heart of God, and moves all things towards wholeness, harmony and perfection.

It is said that time heals all wounds, but that is not always so. Many of us nurse unhealed wounds throughout our lives. Such wounds divert our energies from achieving our full potential and highest expression. Time does not heal all wounds, but love does.

The Angel of Love oversees the highest lesson we can learn: how to love unconditionally – totally, without judgement, question or reservation. Unconditional love is forgiving love, bestowed regardless of circumstance, actions or words. When we are able to love unconditionally, even for a moment, we are one with the Creator.

Unconditional love is sometimes a tall order, especially when we feel aggrieved because of someone else's behaviour. It's human nature to want the gift of our love to change things for the better. Unconditional love teaches us a broader perspective. We must be mindful that loving others unconditionally does not guarantee that we can bring about change in them, or even healing for them. Each soul travels its own path at its own pace. But when we radiate the high vibration of unconditional love, we create an atmosphere that makes positive change easier. The soul, when ready, drinks in the nourishment and it flowers accordingly.

The Angel of Love gently awakens us to the subtle and yet profound workings of the vibration of love. When we invoke the help of this mighty being, our eyes are opened to higher sight.

The Angel of Love also guides us through experience. Once a woman who had been to one of my workshops came up to me and said, 'I really liked your meditation on love, and I thought it would help my relationship with a woman at work who is very mean and rude to me. I've been using the meditation every day for several weeks now, and she's still mean and rude. It hasn't changed her one bit.'

'That's unfortunate,' I said. 'But tell me, how has the meditation changed you?'

The woman thought for a moment. 'You know,' she said, 'it has made me more compassionate towards her. I used to be really angry about the way she treated me, but now I feel rather sorry for her. She must be terribly unhappy inside to put out so much anger. I'm more sympathetic to her than I used to be.'

I nodded. 'Remember that we can only change ourselves – we can't force change on someone else. Love has helped you to transmute your own anger into compassion, which is a tremendous benefit to your own well-being. Your compassion also changes your behaviour, not only towards your angry co-worker, but towards others as well.

'Your co-worker may not be ready to heal her anger and emotional wounds. But at some point, the love and compassion being given to her may suddenly penetrate her heart and she will have an awakening.

'Keep doing the meditation with the help of the Angel of Love,' I said. 'You are raising your spiritual consciousness and helping others to raise theirs, too, simply by the love that you give. We can only offer love, and trust that God will guide it to be used according to the highest purpose. This is how each of us helps to bring about significant change.'

When we give love as unconditionally as we can, we further the work of the Angel of Love. Everything in creation is held together by love. Without love, there would be no order. From love flows out all other virtues. Practising unconditional love enables us to love more fully in many ways, such as loving family and friends, loving what we do, loving humanity and the world of nature, loving God.

MEDITATION

I centre myself in a comfortable position ... I focus attention on my breath, seeing it as light and energy which flows down from the Source through the crown of my head ... filling my body with radiance ... and flowing out through the soles of my feet ... so that I am connected to the inspiration of heaven and the grounding of the earth ... I then breathe in slowly three times ... one breath to relax more deeply and let thoughts and tension drain away ... one breath to centre my attention in stillness ... and one breath to expand my consciousness to the space around me.

I invoke with prayerful and loving intent the presence of my guardian angel and the Angel of Love, to share this journey with me ... assisting me with seeing things in new ways ... and inspiring me to take loving action in the world ... Now before me arise impressions of the Angel of Love ... I take a moment to observe ... and to give thanks for my partnership with the angelic realm.

I bring my total attention to my heart centre ... everything that I am is within the heart in this moment ... I feel the heart ... hear the heart ... become my heart ... the Angel of Love envelops me in soothing light.

From the heart I turn my thoughts to someone I love very deeply ... I allow a name, a face, a presence to rise up spontaneously from the depths of my being ... Gently I hold this person, embraced in my heart ... enfolded in the wings of the Angel of Love ... I send out to them beams of unconditional love ... I wish for them their highest good ... I watch and feel the love go out, taking whatever form it needs ... streams of light ... flowers or stars ... colours ... the love is borne on the wings of the Angel of Love ... I see my love received by the other ... I feel the connection between our two hearts ... we are joined by love that is complete, accepting and ever-giving ... we become love ... I am at total peace.

When I am ready, I release my loved one into the light ... knowing the blessing bestowed will be kept and nourished with the help of the Angel of Love ... I return to my heart ... and take notice of how it is changed and transformed by the expression of unconditional love.

Now I turn my thoughts to someone else ... someone of whom I am fond ... and see that person and hear their name clearly before me in my mind's eye ... The love within me flows out to them ... I send them unconditional love ... wishing for them their highest good ... I watch and feel the love go out, noting the form it takes ... and how it is carried along by the Angel of Love and offered to the one who has arisen in my heart ... I see my love received by the other ... I feel the connection between our two hearts ... we are joined by love that is complete, accepting and ever-giving ... we become love ... I am at total peace.

I release my friend into the light ... blessed and nourished by the Angel of Love ... I return to my heart ... and take notice of how it is changed and transformed by this expression of unconditional love.

When I am ready, I think of another person ... someone I don't get along with or resent ... or feel betrayed by ... or hold a grudge against ... If uncomfortable thoughts arise, I let the Angel of Love take them and purify them and release them into space, sparkling new ... I see this person clearly before me in health and happiness ... The love within me flows out to them ... I send them unconditional love ... wishing for them their highest good ...

accepting them as they are ... forgiving all past hurts ... I watch and feel the love go out, noting the form it takes ... and how it is carried along by the Angel of Love and offered to the one who has arisen in my heart ... I see my love received by the other ... I feel the connection between our two hearts ... we are joined by love that is complete, accepting and ever-giving ... we become love ... I am at total peace.

I release this person into the light ... the Angel of Love wraps me in a glorious, warm light of unconditional love ... I see the light ... I feel the energy flowing around me ... through me ... I feel a great weight lifted from me ... love heals me ... I accept and appreciate everything about myself ... my uniqueness ... my gifts ... the lessons I have learned through my triumphs and also my mistakes ... I fill myself with light ... the light radiates out into infinity ... the essence of who I am merges into the All That Is ... I feel my heart connected to all hearts ... and to the heart of God.

I take three measured breaths ... feeling the breath flow through my body ... reconnecting me to the present moment in time, space and place ... I give thanks to my guardian angel and the Angel of Love for the blessing of this experience ... and I return refreshed from my journey.

Note

If it becomes too difficult to hold your thoughts on the third person, shift back to the first or second person for a moment. Then try again. Don't be discouraged if it seems you 'can't' love a person, even after a few tries. The exercise heals your own wounds and heart, and makes it easier to love others with whom you've had difficulties. Repeat the exercise over time and you will discover that suddenly you have moved into a more loving and charitable consciousness.

The Angel of Patience

Emanates from: Powers

Instant global communications and high-tech living make the pace of life faster and faster – so fast that it seems at times that we can't keep up. We have shorter attention spans and want things to happen more quickly. When they don't, we risk losing our patience.

When patience is lost, balance is lost. Without patience, we are more likely to make decisions that are not in our best interests. We are more likely to treat others poorly. We are more likely to lose sight of where we are and where we are going. St John of Avila had wise words: 'Patience is the guardian of all the other virtues, and, if it fails, we may lose in one moment the labour of many days.'

Life is not a racetrack, but cycles of ebb and flow. Life is a balance of opposites: rest and action; silence and speaking; inspiration and creativity; speed and slowness, growth and decay. How we live within the process of ebb and flow is the key to our fulfilment and happiness. Patience enables us to allow life to unfold in the proper time and manner. Patience enables us to savour and appreciate whatever we are experiencing, at whatever pace.

The Angel of Patience helps us to know how far to go and when to pull back on the reins. There is no denial, no sacrifice. Sometimes we must pause or wait. It may be for something simple, such as waiting our turn longer than we'd like, or waiting for others. It may be for a stage in life, when we don't attain a goal and think we've lost out, when in fact the universe is giving us a needed space for something else to manifest. When we are patient, there are no misses, only opportunities. When we see potential instead of empty spaces, we open the door to an unexpected treasure that has been waiting to come in but could not find the room.

Patience requires self-knowledge and self-control. The more we possess self-knowledge, the better we are able to control our reactions to any given situation. The impatient person is unfairly judgemental. As we reap what we sow, others in turn are unfairly judgemental of us. The impatient person keeps churning out negative emotions of frustration, irritation, anger and disappointment. The patient person generates calmness, peace and an aura of harmony.

Patience also reminds us that to pursue anything in the extreme in order to hurry things up is not a good tactic. We would be wiser to pull back and see the situation from a higher and more detached perspective. Why force a choice for second-best now, when the very best lies down the road?

Draw from all that life has to offer. Compromise, accommodate and be happy. To 'go with the flow' does not mean having no direction or drive. Those who are patient are always in the best control.

MEDITATION

I centre myself in a comfortable position ... I focus attention on my breath, seeing it as light and energy which flows down from the Source through the crown of my head ... filling my body with radiance ... and flowing out through the soles of my feet ... so that I am connected to the inspiration of heaven and the grounding of the earth ... I then breathe in slowly three times ... one breath to relax more deeply and let thoughts and tension drain away ... one breath to centre my attention in stillness ... and one breath to expand my consciousness to the space around me.

I invoke with prayerful and loving intent the presence of my guardian angel and the Angel of Patience, to share this journey with me ... assisting me with seeing things in new ways ... and inspiring me to take loving action in the world ... Now before me arise impressions of the Angel of Patience ... I take a moment to observe

... and to give thanks for my partnership with the angelic realm.

First I look at my patience in my daily life ... and see that I have much room for improvement ... I think of the times I have been frustrated or angry because people did not act as I wanted them to ... or circumstances seemed against me ... I ask the Angel of Patience to send a healing light over those times ... and restore harmony and balance ... I ask for help to have the presence of mind to be patient when I encounter delays and obstacles ... the angel shows me how I can achieve balance by blessing those who try my patience ... I think of people who, for my lack of patience, need a blessing of gratitude from me.

Next I look at my patience in the course and progress of my life ... and I take a few moments to contemplate the matters which make me impatient ... Perhaps I am impatient about starting a new relationship ... or advancing my career ... or being able to make an important decision ... I consider why I am impatient ... I ask for the healing light of patience to be cast over me.

I see how patience is interwoven with faith and trust ... and that if I establish my faith and trust in divine guidance for my highest good ... then patience follows ... I go within to the still and deep part of me ... and breathe in serenity ... knowing that everything now is as it should be ... I understand that patience is action ... that patience means staying the course ... and that sometimes patience and perseverance go hand in hand ... I breathe in serenity.

I am in harmony with the rhythms of life ... I honour the ebb as well as the flow ... I am able to find the positive in life wherever I am.

I take three measured breaths ... feeling the breath flow through my body ... reconnecting me to the present moment in time, space and place ... I give thanks to my guardian angel and the Angel of Patience for the blessing of this experience ... and I return refreshed from my journey.

The Angel of Peace

Emanates from: Principalities

The Angel of Peace works for harmony, balance and love among all living things. On a personal level, the Angel of Peace can help to bring inner peace through the healing of emotions and the resolution of uncertainties, doubts and fears. The Angel of Peace is present whenever we heal relationships and extend love, compassion, understanding and generosity to others. On a grand cosmic scale, the Angel of Peace works to keep all things in creation smoothly meshed together.

We can recognize and invoke the presence of the Angel of Peace with the symbol of the dove. This beautiful, graceful bird with a gentle cooing song seems so sweet and simple, yet it represents a great mystery of tremendous depth and complexity. By its sign, we understand Truth, and when we understand Truth, we establish peace in the heart of the universe.

The Meaning of Doves

Universally, doves – especially white doves – have been associated with purity, innocence, faithfulness, love and peace. They decorate our wedding gifts as symbols of true love and faithful marriage. To the Greeks, doves were Aphrodite's birds, drawing her chariot.

Doves decorate our Christmas and New Year's cards and gifts as symbols of peace, harmony and renewal. Bearing an olive branch, they are our greatest symbol of peace, forgiveness and deliverance. In the biblical story of Noah's ark, deliverance is realized when a dove appears with an olive branch – a sign not only of land nearby and an end to the flood, but of peace between humankind and God.

The dove is a social animal that prefers company. Thus, it represents to us brotherhood among the peoples of the land.

But doves have deeper, more mystical meanings. They are the keepers of secrets and the holders of mysteries. Doves are the fecundating Spirit, and thus are sacred to all Great

Mother Goddesses and Queens of Heaven, including the Blessed Virgin Mary. They are the creative spark that ignites spiritual life within the soul. Doves represent the soul, the imperishable part of the human being.

In the New Testament, a dove appears hovering over the head of Jesus as he is baptized in the River Jordan. The dove signifies the descent of the Divine into the realm of matter, initiating the path back to unity and oneness with All. In sacred art, a dove appears in the Annunciation, representing the fructifying agent of the Holy Ghost and the purity and innocence of Mary as she surrenders to the will of God.

In early Christian legend, a dove descends on the staff of Joseph as a sign to him that he is to marry Mary. Another legend tells that Joachim and Anna, the parents of Mary, dream of a dove before her birth. The Gnostics considered the Holy Ghost to be feminine. They interpreted the dove as Sophia-Sapientia: Wisdom, the wife of God, and the Mother of Christ. They referred to Mary as the *columba mystica*, or 'mystical dove'. Columbia, both a popular name and the mystical name of the United States of America, means 'of the dove'.

The dove figures prominently in legends of the Holy Grail, where it is the symbol of salvation, resurrection and the mystery of the Eucharist. It is the emblem of the Knights of the Grail as they undertake their mystical quest for knowledge of God. In fact, doves accompany many saints and religious figures in story and art.

Doves also represent the souls of the dead, victory over death and renewal of spirit, especially when depicted with a palm branch.

The Dove's Transformation

Whenever we see an image of a dove, or whenever we contemplate the meaning of the dove, a deep part of our consciousness connects to its profound well of sacred and archetypal associations. The sign of the dove, the emissary of the Angel of Peace, activates within us the vibration of peace, love, compassion, creativity and renewal. It fills us with Light. We become channels for the descent of the Divine into us, so that we may bear the fruits of Spirit through all that we think, say and do. The core of our heart opens to the Great Mystery. When we truly live under the sign of the dove, it becomes impossible to hate, steal or kill. We must listen to the gentle song of the dove as it sings to us love ... love ... love ... peace ... peace ... peace.

St Gregory of Nyssa said that the closer the soul approaches the Light, the lovelier it becomes until finally it takes on the form of a dove. Let the dove dwell in your heart, infusing your being with the vibration of the Angel of Peace. Like the dove and the Angel, spread your wings of Truth and soar to the heights. And when all the wings of all the souls on earth are spread on high, their tips will touch and create a magnificent field of radiant love for healing, illumination and peace eternal.

MEDITATION

I centre myself in a comfortable position ... I focus attention on my breath, seeing it as light and energy which
flows down from the Source through the crown of my
head ... filling my body with radiance ... and flowing out
through the soles of my feet ... so that I am connected
to the inspiration of heaven and the grounding of the
earth ... I then breathe in slowly three times ... one
breath to relax more deeply and let thoughts and tension drain away ... one breath to centre my attention in
stillness ... and one breath to expand my consciousness
to the space around me.

I invoke with prayerful and loving intent the presence of
my guardian angel and the Angel of Peace, to share this
journey with me ... assisting me with seeing things in new
ways ... and inspiring me to take loving action in the
world ... Now before me arise impressions of the Angel
of Peace ... I take a moment to observe ... and to give
thanks for my partnership with the angelic realm.

In a sphere of light I behold the radiant Angel of Peace
... soft pastel colours shimmer around us ... we are
together embraced by the beautiful light ... the Angel of
Peace extends as a gift to me a white dove ... the dove

embodies a love so pure that it instantly calms my mind ... my heart opens in the fullness of love and a peace profound ... the energy of this love and peace streams out from my heart ... I see it filling other hearts ... I call to mind now the people and creatures who receive this love, guided to them by the dove of the Angel of Peace ... the energy streams like ribbons of light that flow back into my own heart ... I am connected to the Sacred Circle of Life Eternal and the dove of the Angel of Peace dwells within me.

I take three measured breaths ... feeling the breath flow through my body ... reconnecting me to the present moment in time, space and place ... I give thanks to my guardian angel and the Angel of Peace for the blessing of this experience ... and I return refreshed from my journey.

The Angel of Prayer

Emanates from: Angels

One of the angels' most important functions in building the rainbow bridge of oneness between the human soul and God is acting as the messengers of prayer. Angels carry prayers to God, and carry God's answers back to those who pray.

In rabbinic lore, the giant angel Sandalphon ('co-brother'), the twin brother of Metatron, is charged with weaving human prayers. When Moses ascends to heaven to receive the Torah, he comes upon Sandalphon, whose enormous size strikes fear into his heart. Sandalphon ceaselessly gathers the prayers of Israel and weaves them into garlands, which when completed place themselves on the head of God. Sandalphon is charged with endlessly combatting the dark angel Samael (Satan), a job he shares with the archangel Michael, who also performs duties as the Angel of Prayer. Other angels named as the Angel of Prayer are Gabriel, Raphael and, in Persian lore, Sizouze. Myriads of angels are charged with taking prayers from one level of heaven to another. By asking for the help of the 'Angel of Prayer', we are instantly connected to the angel who is most appropriate for our needs.

It is appropriate that Sandalphon is a giant in stature, for prayer truly is one of the greatest of spiritual powers. Through prayer, we are inspired to make great triumphs, accomplishments and miraculous healings.

In essence, prayer is an act of communing with God. It makes us one with God. The 14th-century mystic Julian of Norwich called prayer 'one-ing with God'. Prayer is the essential link that helps us bridge two worlds – our everyday world and a transcendent reality. In that transcendent world, we see all things as being possible. And we are guided accordingly, to manifest our highest good.

The simplest and most common form of prayer is the petition, in which we ask for something for ourselves. The word 'prayer' itself means to petition, coming from the Latin term *precarius*, which means 'obtained by begging'. Most of us make petitionary prayers on an almost daily basis, informally, whenever we want something to go right in life, or when we want something to change.

Another common form of prayer is intercession, in which we ask for help for another person. Other kinds of prayer are thanksgiving, adoration, confession, lamentation, meditation, contemplation and surrender. Meditation and contemplation are mystical in nature.

Prayer does help us to make change. By asking God for help, we draw upon a vast reservoir of spiritual strength, courage and inspiration. This reservoir permeates the universe. It exists within us as well. In fact, one of the greatest gifts of prayer is that it awakens us to our own inner strength. At times when life looks very dark and grim, prayer provides the lifeline that enables us to persevere, to overcome all obstacles.

The true power and nature of prayer will be brought home to you by shifting your thinking about what is prayer. Think of it as communication and communion with God, but also as a living, dynamic spiritual energy that nourishes us on all levels of our being.

The High Purpose of Prayer

The highest purpose of prayer is to know God – to change our awareness of God so that we express God in all that we think and do. By changing our awareness of God, we change ourselves for the better. We become better channels for the expression of God's virtues in the world. It is certainly all right to ask for things in prayer – we all need divine help – but we should also add to our prayers the simple request to know God and to be at one with God's perfection and harmony.

Knowing God is knowing Truth. God is Truth, and thus Truth is Creator of all that is real. Truth is all that is good.

What Happens When We Pray

A wondrous, marvellous thing happens whenever we engage in prayer, no matter how short or simple. We initiate a flow of spiritual energy into us, into our minds, our hearts, our souls and our bodies. This energy restores, replenishes, strengthens and revitalizes us. What's more, the energy of prayer radiates from us, flowing out to others. We become beacons of divine light and love. We are inspired with new ideas for solutions to problems. We are renewed with strength and determination to overcome obstacles, to reach goals. We are healed. We are filled with love and compassion for others.

Prayer accomplishes many things. It develops our character to its highest state. It builds a mind that is always open to Spirit. Through prayer, we attain an inter-penetrating consciousness with God's perfect life and love and power. Prayer also changes our very energy field, intensifying and brightening the aura of energy around us, which radiates out to have a positive effect on others.

Prayer is one of the most important things we can do for ourselves and for others. Pray for help for your needs, and pray to be lifted up into Oneness with the Creator. The

Angel of Prayer is always watching over us in this most sacred of acts. Whenever you pray, the entire realm of angels rejoices in the reaching out of your heart to God.

All Prayers Are Answered

Sometimes we think that God isn't hearing our prayers, or that his answer to them is 'no'. Neither is the case. God always listens, and the Angel of Prayer takes every prayer, even the smallest, to his attention. God never says 'no'.

There are three fundamental answers to all prayers. The first is 'yes'. The second is 'another way'. The third is 'not yet'. We are never given a flat 'no', nor are we left without support or guidance.

We often don't recognize the second answer, 'another way'. When what we pray for is not forthcoming, this answer tells us to look in another direction. We are always given the opportunity to manifest our highest potential, whether it be through accomplishment, love, forgiveness or even sacrifice. But if we are fixed only on a certain outcome, we will miss the guidance given.

The answer of 'another way' is a reminder to us to stay in attunement with God. If we earnestly seek guidance through prayer, we must be prepared to accept and follow what we receive. We are always given the answer that is in the highest good for each situation. What is in the highest good may be better than what we seek. Or, it may be hard, but necessary, to accept.

We are given a 'not yet' answer when timing is not right, or there are other factors involved:

- We need to release something that is a barrier to moving forward so that the transforming, healing power of God can flow through us. We may unconsciously resist the benefits we seek because of low self-worth, simmering resentments, or even an unclear focus on what we really want.
- There is other work that we need to do in order to bring about the desired results. We've put the cart before the horse, and the answer directs us to re-examine the situation.
- We must take others into account. When we pray for others, their own attunement, beliefs, thoughts, fears, desires and limitations enter into the picture as well. We can send them the healing radiance of prayer, but it is up to them whether to receive and absorb it.

Is there anything that we can't or shouldn't pray for? If we pray for healing, improvement, enlightenment, love, forgiveness, harmony, beauty, peace and Truth – in short, Godly qualities and principles – we will always be in concert with God. We should never use prayer in an attempt to manipulate others or to bring harm to others. Even well-meaning prayer can be manipulative. Otherwise, there is no need too small to address in prayer.

It is fine to pray for specific things or outcomes. We should petition the mighty currents of creation to work for us. But separate your needs from your wants, and pray for what you *need*. If you're not certain what to pray for – especially when praying for others – simply ask for the highest good for all concerned.

If you establish a daily prayer practice, you will find yourself falling into a natural rhythm of prayer, and an awareness of attunement to God that will in turn guide you in your prayers.

MEDITATION

I centre myself in a comfortable position ... I focus attention on my breath, seeing it as light and energy which flows down from the Source through the crown of my head ... filling my body with radiance ... and flowing out through the soles of my feet ... so that I am connected to the inspiration of heaven and the grounding of the earth ... I then breathe in slowly three times ... one breath to relax more deeply and let thoughts and tension drain away ... one breath to centre my attention in stillness ... and one breath to expand my consciousness to the space around me.

I invoke with prayerful and loving intent the presence of my guardian angel and the Angel of Prayer, to share this journey with me ... assisting me with seeing things in new ways ... and inspiring me to take loving action in the world ... Now before me arise impressions of the Angel of Prayer ... I take a moment to observe ... and to give thanks for my partnership with the angelic realm.

I turn my attention to my need, and form a prayer ... I ask the Angel of Prayer to present it to God in a beautiful garland ... I see a garland of lights instantly created ... and borne to the heavens by the Angel ... I know that no request is too small ... no request is too big ... I pray with sincerity and love ... and in faith and certainty that the answer will be given in the moment I make the prayer.

I hold myself open to the answer that serves the highest purpose ... Whatever I am asked to do is within my reach ... my ability ... and my purpose ... In this act of humble prayer, I hear angels sing.

I rest in a space of beauty and peace ... a vessel receiving the divine light of God ... and I pay attention to the thoughts and impressions that arise spontaneously within me ... not judging them ... accepting them ... knowing that they are made known to me with purpose.

The Angel of Prayer appears before me ... bearing me a gift ... it symbolizes the answer ... something I need to know or understand ... something I need to accept ... something I need to do ... I take a few moments now to take the gift ... and give thanks for it ... and observe it with great attention ... I feel wonderful energy radiating from it ... for the gift bears the very essence of love ... just as my answer is given from the Heart of Divine Love.

I know that if I do not understand everything that has been given ... or that if anything remains hidden to me ... that understanding ... and revelation ... will happen at the right place and time ... I take the gift into my heart.

I take three measured breaths ... feeling the breath flow through my body ... reconnecting me to the present moment in time, space and place ... I give thanks to my guardian angel and the Angel of Prayer for the blessing of this experience ... and I return refreshed from my journey.

The Angel of Relationships

Emanates from: Angels

Our greatest treasures in life are our relationships with others. Without bonds, we are but islands in a vast universe. Relationships nourish and inspire us; the human soul thrives on companionship, affection and love.

Sometimes relationships deteriorate in misunderstanding and complex circumstances. Sometimes we project onto relationships something we want, rather than engaging in them as a sharing of spirit.

The Angel of Relationships can lift us to a higher perspective to see relationships in a different light, and to have a greater understanding and appreciation of others.

MEDITATION

I centre myself in a comfortable position ... I focus attention on my breath, seeing it as light and energy which
flows down from the Source through the crown of my
head ... filling my body with radiance ... and flowing out
through the soles of my feet ... so that I am connected
to the inspiration of heaven and the grounding of the
earth ... I then breathe in slowly three times ... one
breath to relax more deeply and let thoughts and tension drain away ... one breath to centre my attention in
stillness ... and one breath to expand my consciousness
to the space around me.

I invoke with prayerful and loving intent the presence of
my guardian angel and the Angel of Relationships, to
share this journey with me ... assisting me with seeing
things in new ways ... and inspiring me to take loving
action in the world ... Now before me arise impressions
of the Angel of Relationships ... I take a moment to
observe ... and to give thanks for my partnership with
the angelic realm.

I see myself surrounded by the happy images of people
I know ... the truth arises within me that these souls care
deeply about me ... and I care about them ... the love and

care that flows among us shimmers like cords of light ... the cords are held by the Angel of Relationships ... there are many cords for many kinds of relationships ... friendship ... family ... romantic love ... brotherly love ... neighbourhood and community ... teamwork in work ... care-giving ... planetary citizenship ... I take a moment to experience the many kinds of my relationships as they rise to my attention spontaneously.

I am opened to a new understanding of my relationships ... The Angel of Relationships tends the cords, but it is I through my free will who determines whether they are strengthened or damaged ... I listen to the Angel, whose thoughts are impressed upon me as my own, a part of me ... and I understand how I can work with the Angel of Relationships to bring the powers of earth and heaven together to strengthen the bonds between me and all things.

I am shown a vast network of souls who care immensely about me ... as I experience their feelings I understand the depths of every relationship, no matter how informal or casual it may appear to be ... I am directed to think again of individuals I know ... beginning with those for whom I care the most ... and contemplate how they have touched my life. I look into the Angel's face as I turn my thoughts to the names and faces that arise before me ... I am filled with gratitude that all of them have agreed to be with me, here and now ... The Angel of Relationships

directs my attention to the potential that each relationship has to rise to a greater and higher level ... possibilities dance before me ... I feel I am seeing through the
eyes of the Angel the highest and greatest good that
ever presents itself in opportunities and choices ... I am
as in a dream ... a dream that is very real and I am quiet-
ed by the moment.

Gratitude flows through me for those with whom I have
crossed only minor paths ... I see that the people who
built the roads on which I tread have contributed signifi-
cantly to my life ... I see that my teachers who shared
their dreams with me in their vision of what I could
become have added today to who I am now ... Others,
whom I have experienced through heartache and pain,
have shown me both where I need to be and also where
I do not need to be.

All these experiences now become a lesson ... I see that
they were designed to teach me to walk towards happiness ... When I know a road is bad, I will naturally not
take it ... Because I remember so vividly, I now have
gained wisdom ... What I now want becomes clearer ...
and what I have learned becomes obvious.

The Angel of Relationships tells me, 'You are here to
experience, and experience cannot be told ... In your
relationships with others you perform the work you
planned with God. Others in their relationship with you

experience their work with God ... God begins as a friend, becomes a loved one and finally elevates you to everlasting union with him.'

Out of the quiet of these thoughts I hear a gentle sound of nature in the distance ... the warmth of the sun bathes me ... I am at peace ... my work with the angelic realm and my work with God takes on new direction ... new meaning ... In this moment, right now, I am touched in the depths of my being.

I take three measured breaths ... feeling the breath flow through my body ... reconnecting me to the present moment in time, space and place ... I give thanks to my guardian angel and the Angel of Relationships for the blessing of this experience ... and I return refreshed from my journey.

The Angel of Release

Emanates from: Archangels

Life isn't always a smooth journey. Were it only so! Sometimes just when we think things are going well, we have a setback. Sometimes we think we're doing all we can to move forward, but progress is slow – or sometimes non-existent.

The solution to our situation may be that we need to let go of something that no longer has a place in our life. It might be a relationship. It might be a job. It might be an attachment to certain values or things, or to outcomes of situations. It might be an old hurt. It might be fear. Or doubt.

Sometimes we even become attached to illness as a way of not having to do other things, or prove our ability to succeed. True healing cannot take place if we hold on to an illness or problem. On a deep level of consciousness, some people do not wish to be healed. Perhaps they get attention as a result of their illness, or perhaps they can avoid certain responsibilities. All healing involves a willingness to let go of pain or a problem.

All of the major spiritual traditions teach the importance of releasing our attachments to things and desires in the material plane before we can truly access Spirit. When we pray, especially for certain goals and objectives, we must detach ourselves from the outcome, placing the matter in the hands of God. We don't know what is best for us in the long run, let alone what is good for another person. Yet we pray as though we do know what's best. The big picture, constructed by the Master Architect, is not visible to us. We see only tiny portions of it.

Our Higher Self knows when we need to let go, even if we're not even sure what it is that needs to be released. Sometimes it's not easy. When something that has filled our energetic space is released, it creates a space to be filled. We might unknowingly fear what will come into that space. The unknown new might be challenging, difficult to handle.

Calling on the Angel of Release can help us make the turning-point.

MEDITATION

I centre myself in a comfortable position ... I focus attention on my breath, seeing it as light and energy which
flows down from the Source through the crown of my
head ... filling my body with radiance ... and flowing out
through the soles of my feet ... so that I am connected
to the inspiration of heaven and the grounding of the
earth ... I then breathe in slowly three times ... one
breath to relax more deeply and let thoughts and tension drain away ... one breath to centre my attention in
stillness ... and one breath to expand my consciousness
to the space around me.

I invoke with prayerful and loving intent my guardian
angel and the presence of the Angel of Release, to
share this journey with me ... assisting me with seeing
things in new ways ... and inspiring me to take loving
action in the world ... Now before me arise impressions
of the Angel of Release ... I take a moment to observe ...
and to give thanks for my partnership with the angelic
realm.

I notice that I am weighed down ... the unwanted and unneeded cling to me ... making my steps heavy ... and my effort great ... What is it that weighs me down? ... and holds me back? ... I ask to be purified, healed and made an instrument for God ... I know that these are the conditions of true change ... The Angel of Release takes me to a series of three gateways ... the gateways lead to higher planes of consciousness ... through them I can shed my weights of things and cares I no longer need.

The first gateway is humility ... I realize I do not know all the answers ... I cannot expect to control everything around me ... a greater plan is at work in the universe ... I am an important part of that plan ... I understand that in order to grow, I must release rigid ideas and concepts of who I am.

My thoughts turn to the weight I know I must release ... its purpose has been fulfilled ... I desire to release it now with all my heart ... I visualize this weight ... feel it ... and when I let it go, the Angel of Release takes it and gently sends it away into divine light.

My thoughts turn to hidden weights ... things that hold me back but which have not been acknowledged by me ... I ask the Angel of Release to show me what else I need to release ... trusting in the guidance as right and meaningful ... I allow thoughts and impressions to rise spontaneously within me ... not judging them ... but accepting them ... I ask the Angel for any help I need ... I see the weights as stones in my hands ... I open my hands and let the stones go ... into the light.

The second gateway is surrender ... I surrender to a power greater than myself ... and in this surrender comes a liberation ... a triumph ... for I am raised to a higher vibration of awareness ... I surrender to the unfoldment of the divine plan ... I ask the Angel of Release to show me what I need to nourish now in my new space ... to show me the unfoldment of my Becoming ... Lighter and brighter, I am ready to embrace something new ... gone are fears and uncertainties ... I welcome in faith, trust, strength and vision.

The third gateway is rebirth ... it is an arc of rainbow light that stretches across infinity ... I celebrate my Becoming ... and the angelic kingdom rejoices with me ... the death of the old through my release now makes possible the birth of something new and wonderful within me ... I embrace the new ... I see and feel changes within me ... they come into my awareness.

The Angel of Release brings forward a new spiritual body for me ... a garment of light ... and I put it on ... it is the garment of the Courage to Change ... to leave behind what no longer serves my purpose or God's purpose ... and to move forward on a new path of light.

That path of light reveals itself before me ... I know that I will not always see what lies ahead ... but I trust in the journey.

I take three measured breaths ... feeling the breath flow through my body ... reconnecting me to the present moment in time, space and place ... I give thanks to my guardian angel and the Angel of Release for the blessing of this experience ... and I return refreshed from my journey.

The Angel of Solutions

Emanates from: Principalities

Do you ever feel that problems literally have tied you up in knots? And that things have become so convoluted that you feel you can't possibly find a solution? There is an answer to every question, problem or dilemma – all you have to do to find it is 'pull the string' held by the Angel of Solutions.

Every knot has a loose end. When you find it and follow it, you can unravel even the trickiest knot. So it is with problems. There always is a solution that will unravel the most difficult of situations.

When something is knotted, we often attack the knot in annoyance or frustration. We yank this way and that to untie the knot as quickly as possible. Sometimes pulling too hard on what looks like a loose end only makes the knot worse.

The same thing happens with problems. We want instant solutions. We want to attack the problem and get it fixed immediately. Or, we're overwhelmed and think it can't be fixed, and we give up or walk away. We toss it out, like a ball of yarn that seems hopelessly knotted.

We can unravel difficult knots only if we have patience. Similarly, solving problems in life requires patience, too. The loose end always will lead to the heart of the matter. Sometimes it doesn't seem obvious. But if we follow the thread gently, it straightens out.

Our solutions will also be quicker and smoother if we change our attitude. Irritation over a problem creates a field of negative energy around us. If we bless the problem, we infuse the situation with divine healing energy.

MEDITATION

I centre myself in a comfortable position ... I focus attention on my breath, seeing it as light and energy which flows down from the Source through the crown of my head ... filling my body with radiance ... and flowing out through the soles of my feet ... so that I am connected to the inspiration of heaven and the grounding of the earth ... I then breathe in slowly three times ... one breath to relax more deeply and let thoughts and tension drain away ... one breath to centre my attention in stillness ... and one breath to expand my consciousness to the space around me.

I invoke with prayerful and loving intent the presence of my guardian angel and the Angel of Solutions, to share this journey with me ... assisting me with seeing things in new ways ... and inspiring me to take loving action in the world ... Now before me arise impressions of the Angel of Solutions ... I take a moment to observe ... and to give thanks for my partnership with the angelic realm.

I focus on the nature and quality of my thoughts and feelings ... I acknowledge any frustration, resentment, anger or other negative feelings that have arisen in me in response to my situation ... I release these feelings ... letting them dissolve in showers of light ... I give thanks for the problem ... which I now see is not a difficulty, but an opportunity for spiritual growth.

I hold in my mind's eye a knotted ball of golden cord ... this knotted ball represents my problem ... the Angel of Solutions tells me to look closer ... and I see that a loose end of cord sticks out from the ball ... the loose end is brightly lit ... a gentle glow surrounds it ... this is the path to my solution ... I know that the Angel cannot give me the solution ... I must unravel it myself ... the Angel stands ready to guide and help me.

I take the loose end, and gently start working on the knot ... knowing that I am now solving my problem ... I am guided in accordance to my highest good and the highest good of all ... I accept that within me is everything I need to know to arrive at the right solution ... I trust the guidance ... I trust the unfoldment.

As I unravel the cord ... thoughts and impressions come to me ... I pay attention ... if they do not make immediate sense, I know that I will understand them at the right and perfect time ... I ask the Angel of Solutions to help me see and understand all sides of the matter ... and to know beyond doubt the right solution.

The knotted ball is now unravelled ... the shining cord is straight and true ... I feel a well-being and certainty deep within me ... Even if the answer has not come with clarity, I know that I have done the work in good faith ... and that all the pieces will fall into place ... I know that further insights may come in my dreams ... in intuitive thoughts that arise during the day ... in the words of others ... in signs ... and in moments of inspiration ... I give thanks for the answer ... which I feel within me as a beautiful light.

I take three measured breaths ... feeling the breath flow through my body ... reconnecting me to the present moment in time, space and place ... I give thanks to my guardian angel and the Angel of Solutions for the blessing of this experience ... and I return refreshed from my journey.

At last your knot unravels. What is inside, at the centre? Perhaps you find an object that pertains to your solution. Perhaps you find a golden ball of light – the light of illumination.

Record your experience, including the thoughts and images that came to you while you were undoing the knot. The meaning of some may not be readily apparent, but will be revealed later.

Stay alert for more inspiration. Ideas and solutions sometimes unfold in stages. You may get part of the answer now, part later. Pay attention to synchronistic events, and to your dreams.

Remember that every problem, every dilemma, not only has a solution, but has the right solution. The solution may be hidden in a knot of confusion, but it can always be found. Follow the thread, follow the lead, follow the idea, follow the guidance. And suddenly there you are, in the centre of clear understanding!

The Angel of Strength

Emanates from: Powers

From an early age, we learn that life will present difficulties. Experience quickly teaches us that we must develop inner strength if we are to persevere and live life to its fullest. Our inner strength enables us to face up to the questions in our lives, to cope with changes, overcome trials, and to carry on.

Strength is powered by the belief we have in ourselves and our faith in divine will. The more we believe in ourselves and our abilities, the more the barriers will fall. The greater our trust and faith in divine guidance, the greater is our strength to triumph over any adversity.

A strong person keeps emotions in balance. Strength is reflected outwards in a serenity that is noticeable to others, and has a calming effect. When we draw upon inner strength, we see through eyes of wisdom. We learn from mistakes and become stronger and better. Strength gives us toughness and intensity, and enables us to have courage.

In any given situation, we find our strength in our own ways. We may automatically pray a certain prayer. We may call forth a mental image that is personally significant to us. Whatever our way, the Angel of Strength immediately attunes us to our divinely guided power. If we ever face dire circumstances, the immediate flow of inner strength enables us to perform acts of heroism.

When terrorists hijacked four aeroplanes in the United States on September 11, 2001, the passengers on board faced terrifying, unimaginable circumstances. We will never know how many of them responded, but we do have records of what took place aboard one of the planes. The passengers on United Airlines Flight 93 summoned their strength and their courage to overcome the hijackers with the help of a well-known prayer: the Lord's Prayer.

Flight 93 was eastbound on a routine transcontinental flight that fateful morning when the hijackers seized control of the cockpit and turned it towards Washington, DC. Via mobile phones, the passengers learned of the three other hijacked planes that were crashed into the World Trade Centre and the Pentagon. They resolved not to allow the hijackers of their plane to commit a similar atrocity. They decided to attack their captors. The last thing they did together was say the Lord's Prayer. It helped them to cast away fear and find their strength and resolve.

Minutes after a group of the passengers stormed the hijackers in the cockpit, the jet crashed in a field in Pennsylvania, killing all on board – but preventing the horrible death and destruction intended by the hijackers. Those brave passengers sacrificed their lives to save many others.

Countless people all over the world, and from diverse religions, call upon the Lord's Prayer when they need strength in times of crisis and need. What is it about the Lord's Prayer that is so powerful?

The 'Our Father', as the Lord's Prayer is also called, was delivered by Jesus in his Sermon on the Mount, when he instructed people how to pray, as recorded in Matthew 6:7. But the power of the Lord's Prayer transcends any denominational label.

St John Cassian, a monk and a father of the Church, called the Lord's Prayer 'the prayer of fire'. This prayer, John says in his great work, *Conferences*, 'contains all the fullness of perfection, inasmuch as the Lord himself has given it to us, both as a model and also as a precept. Those who are familiar with this prayer are raised by it to a very lofty condition, namely that "prayer of fire" which very few know by direct experience and which it is impossible to describe.'

John continues, 'The "prayer of fire" transcends all human feeling. There are no longer sounds of the voice nor movements of the tongue nor articulated words. The soul is completely imbued with divine light. Human language, always inadequate, is no use any more. But in the soul is a spring bubbling over, and prayer gushing out from it leaps up to God. The soul expresses in a single instant many things which could only be described or remembered with difficulty when it has returned to its normal condition.'

The Lord's Prayer is a 'prayer of fire' because it moves human consciousness up from the material and into a higher spiritual consciousness. Enlightened by divine light, the soul is able to reach into its depths and call up the strength, the power and the courage to do what is right and to endure trials. The 'prayer of fire' unites the soul to God in a wordless knowing.

The Lord's Prayer acquires much of its power from the fact that millions of souls have spoken it, thought it and believed in it for two millennia. Every time it is used, it is energized.

The Lord's Prayer is by no means the only 'prayer of fire'. Every faith, every spiritual tradition has its special prayers that act in the same way. A prayer used over and over again by many people accumulates great energy and force.

The key to benefiting from the power of prayer is faith. A dry repetition makes no prayer a 'prayer of fire'. But a deep desire to reach God, a desire for true strength, and a faith in the power of a prayer to establish that connection all serve to ignite the brilliant fire of divine light within us.

For the passengers on Flight 93, the Lord's Prayer helped them in a critical moment of trial. Though few of us will ever look the same crisis in the eye as did they, we nonetheless face our own trials in daily life, and often doubt our strength and ability to overcome them.

Seek now to cast away doubt, and find your own 'prayer of fire' that enables you to feel the strength of God within you. Your prayer of fire may be a prayer, or it may be distilled in an image – for example, a heart.

MEDITATION

I centre myself in a comfortable position ... I focus attention on my breath, seeing it as light and energy which flows down from the Source through the crown of my head ... filling my body with radiance ... and flowing out through the soles of my feet ... so that I am connected to the inspiration of heaven and the grounding of the earth ... I then breathe in slowly three times ... one breath to relax more deeply and let thoughts and tension drain away ... one breath to centre my attention in stillness ... and one breath to expand my consciousness to the space around me.

I invoke with prayerful and loving intent the presence of my guardian angel and the Angel of Strength, to share this journey with me ... assisting me with seeing things in new ways ... and inspiring me to take loving action in the world ... Now before me arise impressions of the Angel of Strength ... I take a moment to observe ... and to give thanks for my partnership with the angelic realm.

I acknowledge that many times in life I have wondered if I had the strength to face what lay before me ... and when I could not feel my strength within me I thought of giving up ... I have had setbacks and defeats ... and I have had successes and victories ... I see now that both involve strength ... for strength is about going the distance ... and strength is about summoning the most noble part of me to act in faith and trust in divine will.

I ask the Angel of Strength to reveal to me knowledge of my own strength ... and as soon as I ask I see a vision of myself ... My mouth opens and a stream of light pours into me ... filling every pore and cell of my being ... This light is God's grace, power, presence and will ... the angel shows me that I partake of this essence and presence with every breath that goes into my body ... The breath of God carries divine strength ... it has always been a part of me ... and always will be a part of me.

The Angel of Strength now shows me times in which I have been strong ... for myself ... for others ... for ideals and principles ... perhaps I have forgotten some of them ... or I had not seen those times as evidence of my own strength ... and I take some time now to see those scenes ... and understand more the God-powered strength within me.

I ask to be shown my own 'prayer of fire' ... the word, symbol, image, affirmation or prayer that will instantly empower me to act from true strength ... It rises spontaneously within me.

I am aware now that my breath is the breath of God and God's strength ... and I automatically have all the inner resources I will ever need in any situation ... I think now of a present need for strength ... and ask to be shown how I should use my strength.

With my prayer of fire vividly in my mind and heart ... I embrace my true strength.

I take three measured breaths ... feeling the breath flow through my body ... reconnecting me to the present moment in time, space and place ... I give thanks to my guardian angel and the Angel of Strength for the blessing of this experience ... and I return refreshed from my journey.

The Angel of Thanksgiving

Emanates from: Virtues

Thanksgiving is one of life's arts that often gets overlooked. We rush through busy days and busy lives, pulled this way and that. Sometimes it seems that more things go wrong than go right, and we grumble about our luck or our lot in life, and ask, 'Why can't things be better?' or 'What did I do to deserve this?' Yet it takes only a small turn of the head to see life from the perspective that, rain or shine, all is well and as it should be.

We often give our thanks in routine ways: a blessing said quickly at a meal, a passing grateful thought that circumstances work to our advantage. We are more attentive in our thanks when we express our love and appreciation to others in letters, notes and gifts, and in our devotion to God in worship.

True thanksgiving goes much deeper. True thanksgiving is meant to be a fundamental awareness in life, part of our cellular consciousness. It is our appreciation, our gratitude, for dancing in God's glorious creation – our joy at the fact that we simply *are*.

True thanksgiving appreciates all of life's experiences, from the highs to the lows. Everything is part of our unfoldment. When we learn to embody thankfulness, we attract more positive circumstances to us. We learn to make the most of everything. Life is short, and life is precious.

St Faustina Kowalska captured the essence of thanksgiving in her autobiography *Divine Mercy in My Soul*, in which she describes an epiphany during prayer:

> *My spirit engrossed itself in the benefits that God has lavished on me throughout this whole year. My soul trembled at the sight of this immensity of God's graces. From my soul there burst forth a hymn of thanksgiving to the Lord. For a whole hour, I remained steeped in adoration and thanksgiving, contemplating, one by one, the benefits I had received from God and also my own minor shortcomings. All that this year contained has gone into the abyss of eternity. Nothing is lost. I am glad that nothing gets lost.*

Nothing is ever lost; everything can be turned into something new and good. True thanksgiving is like rain falling upon ready soil – it nourishes the growth of prosperity itself. There is nothing like appreciation, love, praise and thanksgiving to increase our abundance. The more we praise and give thanks, the greater will be the outpouring of the riches of the heavenly kingdom.

MEDITATION

I centre myself in a comfortable position ... I focus attention on my breath, seeing it as light and energy which flows down from the Source through the crown of my head ... filling my body with radiance ... and flowing out through the soles of my feet ... so that I am connected to the inspiration of heaven and the grounding of the earth ... I then breathe in slowly three times ... one breath to relax more deeply and let thoughts and tension drain away ... one breath to centre my attention in stillness ... and one breath to expand my consciousness to the space around me.

I invoke with prayerful and loving intent the presence of my guardian angel and the Angel of Thanksgiving, to share this journey with me ... assisting me with seeing things in new ways ... and inspiring me to take loving action in the world ... Now before me arise impressions of the Angel of Thanksgiving ... I take a moment to observe ... and to give thanks for my partnership with the angelic realm.

Praise and joy and blessing fill my mind, body and life ... I bless the souls who come into my life ... I am thankful for all that I have ... I give thanks for the answers to my prayers ... and know that the answers are in concert with divine order ... working out for the highest good of all concerned.

I call to mind one thing for which I am deeply and profoundly grateful ... something that makes life matter to me ... and I bathe it in a glow of love.

I call to mind a problem present in my life ... a difficult person or relationship ... something that frustrates me ... vexes me ... or even creates a great deal of turmoil for me ... Perhaps I have resented this problem ... I ask the Angel of Thanksgiving to help me transform my attitude ... to see the situation from a higher and better perspective ... The Angel touches my brow and I am infused with a loving warmth.

I find within me the ability to give thanks for this problem ... to be grateful it has come into my life ... for it brings an opportunity for me to grow ... to change ... to heal ... to become a better person ... a more enlightened soul ... I see this problem now in a glow of love ... and know that I can transform it with divine help.

Everything in life has an opposite ... and if I look to the opposite end of the problem ... I see happiness ... harmony ... balance ... and well-being ... The place in-between is the path from one to the other.

I am thankful for every day ... for every breath ... for the sun that rises and the moon that glows in the night ... I am thankful for everything that exists in the spectacular hand of God ... and to be a part of it ... Like a sunflower I open into great beauty when I turn my face towards God.

I resolve that every day I will honour thanksgiving ... I will give thanks when I rise ... even if for but one small thing ... and I will give thanks when I prepare to sleep ... even if for another small thing ... For I know that thanksgivings grow and multiply ... and attract blessings ... so that soon life is lit with joy ... and shadows are banished.

I take three measured breaths ... feeling the breath flow through my body ... reconnecting me to the present moment in time, space and place ... I give thanks to my guardian angel and the Angel of Thanksgiving for the blessing of this experience ... and I return refreshed from my journey.

The Angel of Truth

Emanates from: Cherubim

The spiritual journey is one to find Truth. We want to know what Truth is, yet we discover that it defies word and reason. It is a mystery, tended by angels, that can be known only through experience.

We can, however, grasp some of the essence of Truth. God is Truth, and thus Truth is Creator of all that is real. There is only one mind, the mind of God, and each person is a unique expression of that Universal Mind.

Jesus talked about the Spirit of Truth as a force that represents God and dwells within. 'If you love me, you will keep my commandments,' Jesus said. 'And I will pray to the Father, and he will give you another Counsellor, to be with you forever, even the Spirit of truth, whom the world cannot receive, because it neither sees him or knows him; you know him, for he dwells with you, and will be in you,' he said in John 14:15-17. When the Spirit of Truth comes – that is, when we awaken – we are guided into 'all the truth', as Jesus said in John 16:13.

Understanding Truth is an experience unique to each person. No person can tell another what is Truth. It must be discovered for yourself in your own spiritual journey. Sometimes we try too hard to discover and understand Truth. We want to know it all at once. Truth is an unfoldment – it comes to us naturally. It resides in the heart. The more we pray, the greater unfolding awareness we have of Truth.

We sometimes try too hard to perceive Truth instead of allowing it to unfold. The Spirit of Truth gives us a right understanding of all we experience, and helps us to call upon our powers to meet every need. If we strive to live to the highest principles, we embody Truth, and by embodying it, we understand it.

We also can find Truth by disciplining the mind. We do this by retraining our thinking to eliminate negative, counter-productive thoughts. A mind filled with turbulent, angry, fearful, negative thoughts cannot be reached by the divine Mind. Rather, we should be full of positive thoughts of praise and thanksgiving, love and faith. This establishes a field of loving light around us, and we become a magnet to attract every good and soul-satisfying thing. The most important way to discipline the mind, and thus connect with Truth, is to spend regular time in prayer and meditation.

Mental discipline is built up just like physical muscle: regular exercise strengthens it and increases its power. Through mental discipline, we are able to still the mind in order to hear the voice of God.

Improving our thoughts automatically affects our words for the better. Our thoughts and words really are one. If we think in alignment with God, then we speak in alignment with God as well. And when we are in alignment with God, we become the expressions of perfect love. As St Paul observed, we exhibit patience, kindness, generosity, contentment, modesty, goodness and good temper, truth, burden-bearing capacity, faith in everything, a hope for the happy outcome of everything, and never a thought of failure. Perfect love casts away all fear. It is fear that limits us and narrows our vision.

Especially powerful moments are experienced in a meditative state of prayer called 'the Silence'. When we sit in the Silence, we become receptacles, or holy grails, to be filled with the divine Mind. In the Silence, we are inspired with fresh resolve, with new creative thought, with solutions to problems and with the understandings of Truth that we need.

Mental discipline must be followed by positive action – we must live the thoughts and ideals held within the consciousness. We also discipline the mind by focusing our attention in the here and now. Expressing joy and divine love unifies our heart and mind and strengthens our trust with God.

The Angel of Truth speaks no words, but reveals much.

MEDITATION

I centre myself in a comfortable position ... I focus attention on my breath, seeing it as light and energy which flows down from the Source through the crown of my head ... filling my body with radiance ... and flowing out through the soles of my feet ... so that I am connected to the inspiration of heaven and the grounding of the earth ... I then breathe in slowly three times ... one breath to relax more deeply and let thoughts and tension drain away ... one breath to centre my attention in stillness ... and one breath to expand my consciousness to the space around me.

I invoke with prayerful and loving intent the presence of my guardian angel and the Angel of Truth, to share this journey with me ... assisting me with seeing things in new ways ... and inspiring me to take loving action in the world ... Now before me arise impressions of the Angel of Truth ... I take a moment to observe ... and to give thanks for my partnership with the angelic realm.

I look out into space and see before me my path of light ... it winds through the cosmos like a brilliant ribbon ... I cannot see the end, for there is no end ... the journey unfolds into the ever-new ... my place in the cosmos is eternal.

The path is overlighted by the Angel of Truth ... whose presence is large beyond knowing ... powerful beyond knowing ... The Angel of Truth takes many forms ... I see the Angel in my own likeness ... From this mighty being come three rays of light ... one ray from each hand and one ray from the brow, the centre of the spiritual eye ... The rays weave into me ... connecting me to the Source of Truth ... the Unknowable ... the Ineffable.

I am in a golden globe of light ... a drop of life in an ocean of cosmic love ... Questions rise up within me ... What is my Truth? ... as a soul? ... as part of God? ... in this life? ... How can I understand Truth? ... How can I embody Truth in my life?

The answers are written by God upon my heart ... they have always been there ... life after life I discover them ... one by one ... again in different ways ... and my discovery illuminates the light of my soul.

In the still and silent point within ... at the very heart of creation ... I rest ... light as a feather ... in perfect peace ... in perfect love ... made like a vessel ... for the gold of God to be poured forth into me.

Truth flows in me ... Truth flows through me ... Truth flows from me ... I live and walk and breathe in the Spirit of Truth ... sometimes Truth is revealed in subtle ways ... sometimes in direct ways.

The Angel of Truth holds up a mirror ... what I see in it depends upon my perspective ... this way it is black and bottomless, as fathomless as the Mystery itself ... that way I see things behind me I have not seen before ... another way I myself as I really am ... and yet another way get a glimpse of my Becoming.

The vessel I am ... holds Truth in perfection ... love in perfection ... My understanding is as vast as the canopy of infinite stars before me.

I take three measured breaths ... feeling the breath flow through my body ... reconnecting me to the present moment in time, space and place ... I give thanks to my guardian angel and the Angel of Truth for the blessing of this experience ... and I return refreshed from my journey.

The Angel of Will

Emanates from: Virtues

My will – or thy will?

Sometimes life seems a constant battle of wills. We pit our will against adversity and obstacles. We use will to overcome temptation, and to persevere to a goal. We match our will against the wills of others, determined to come out the stronger party and prevail with our agendas and desires. We ask for the will of God to help us in our quests.

Without will, we would accomplish little. Life would be unorganized. Dreams would go unrealized.

But as we turn inward in the spiritual life, another force comes into play: God's will as the guiding light of life itself.

It's a natural struggle to place our will second to that of God. God's will can seem remote and lofty, even unknowable; meanwhile, we here on earth must struggle with the affairs of daily life and obligations.

To keep a clear perspective, we can call upon the Angel of Will. Think of this angel as similar to the angel who holds the scales of justice. There is balance between the will of the soul and the will of God. The Angel of Will is charged with helping souls see this balance, and maintains it in their material and spiritual life.

Knowing God's Will

A pivotal point in the ministry of Jesus took place after the Last Supper, when Jesus prayed at Gethsemane. Knowing what lay before him, Jesus asked his Father to 'let this cup pass' from him. But at the same time, he acknowledged that whatever happened would not be according to his will, but to God's will.

From this event we take our instruction on the importance of following God's will. It isn't easy. We spend a lot of time trying to figure out what God's will is, and then trying to resolve the struggle between our will and divine will.

How can we know what God's will is? How does it make itself evident?

Scripture associates God's will with moral law, which human beings are charged to follow through their own volition and co-operation. Jesus talked about God's will, but did not define it. The saints and theologians who came after him equated it with everything that is good, righteous and perfect – all of which are subjective in nature. That doesn't help us much when we are faced with a situation that has several good alternatives. Which one is the right one, the one that God wills?

Following God's will becomes much easier if we change our focus. God's will is not concerned with micro-managing daily affairs. Rather, God's will is vast in scope, operating on a much higher level. It can be defined by one word: oneness. God's will is oneness. And oneness is achieved through love.

Actually, we are never *not* doing God's will. God's will is not something you 'try' to do one day, and you don't do another day. You cannot escape God's will. It is a part of you and you are a part of it. The real question is, how well you are doing God's will?

As long as you think of God's will as something separate from yourself, you will remain apart from Oneness. As long as you see God's will as something you have to surrender to as though you and God were in a constant wrestling match, you will remain apart from Oneness.

Jesus' prayer teaches us a deeper understanding of Oneness. When Jesus said, 'not as I will but as thou wilt', he expressed the total acceptance and understanding of his profound statement recorded in John 10:30: 'I and the Father are one.' Thus, there is no separation of wills. In that moment of prayer at Gethsemane, he accepted the unfoldment of his destiny for the fulfilment of divine purpose.

The choice was his to make. The fulfilment of his divine purpose to the best of his ability was very clear.

But our choices are not always so clear. Sometimes we

must choose among options that all seem good, and in which no moral laws are violated. In truth, God's will is never entirely revealed to us, and often there are myriad ways in which to follow God's will. That puts a lot of responsibility on us. We must use discernment. We should not try to break our will but strengthen it through prayer, meditation and spiritual study.

Rather than ask, 'What is God's will?' ask yourself, 'How can I best serve Oneness through love?'

MEDITATION

I centre myself in a comfortable position ... I focus attention on my breath, seeing it as light and energy which flows down from the Source through the crown of my head ... filling my body with radiance ... and flowing out through the soles of my feet ... so that I am connected to the inspiration of heaven and the grounding of the earth ... I then breathe in slowly three times ... one breath to relax more deeply and let thoughts and tension drain away ... one breath to centre my attention in stillness ... and one breath to expand my consciousness to the space around me.

I invoke with prayerful and loving intent the presence of my guardian angel and the Angel of Will, to share this journey with me ... assisting me with seeing things in new ways ... and inspiring me to take loving action in the world ... Now before me arise impressions of the Angel of Will ... I take a moment to observe ... and to give thanks for my partnership with the angelic realm.

From the Angel of Will I feel tremendous strength ... unbreakable strength ... but strength that is flexible ... and bends with the curve and flow of the universe ... For will operates in accordance with the highest good ... From Oneness stream the creative forces that make up the planes of heaven and the planes of worlds ... everything is in constant motion ... but all united in the One ... all serving the One.

The Angel of Will shows me that a strong will is good ... a strong will is an asset in life ... a strong will is valuable in the spiritual struggle of light against darkness ... It is how we use our will that is important ... the will of the Creator works through the wills of the many.

I ask the Angel of Will to show me how I should use my will for the highest good in my life ... the answers of the Angel unfold before me in images, words, impressions and feelings ... I rest in this space to absorb the teaching.

I ask the Angel of Will to show me how I can best serve Oneness through love ... again come answers in pictures, words, sounds, emotions and impressions ... the energy penetrates me so that I take it deep into my being ... my understanding is clear.

I ask for the Angel of Will to take up residence in my heart ... so that God, through the ministering of his angel, will ever guide and make known to me the unfoldment of will that serves Oneness through love.

I take three measured breaths ... feeling the breath flow through my body ... reconnecting me to the present moment in time, space and place ... I give thanks to my guardian angel and the Angel of Will for the blessing of this experience ... and I return refreshed from my journey.

The Angel of Words

Emanates from: Archangels

In childhood we learned the self-defence rhyme of 'Sticks and stones may break my bones but names will never hurt me.' Despite the bravado in that, we know differently, even as children: names – and words – can indeed hurt us. They don't break our physical bones, but they can break our spiritual bones. The bones that carry our self-esteem. Our pride.

Our confidence. Our ability to love. Words that bring us down ring within us for years after they've been spoken.

Even though we know first-hand the ability of words to harm, we still are often thoughtless about our choices of words. Words fly off our tongues, and if we regret them we try to apologize for them, even though we can never really take them back.

When we enter the spiritual path, we begin to change our actions as we seek to help others. And when we learn about the power of thought to create, we become mindful of our thoughts.

The words we choose reflect our true nature. 'Words are truly the images of the soul,' said St Basil the Great in one of the hundreds of letters he wrote during his lifetime as a leader in the early Church. Are your words reflecting the image you'd like to have – or think you have?

The spoken word has a powerful impact. Words create. Spiritual traditions around the world – including our own – tell of creation itself coming from sound and words. In Genesis, God creates by saying, 'Let there be light.' The Gospel of John begins, 'In the beginning was the Word,' and it is the Word of God that brings forth the world. In Egyptian mythology, creation begins when the first god, Ra, emerges from primordial chaos by speaking his name. We say the names of God in mantras and prayers in order to absorb the vibration of God deep into our being.

The power of words works on us daily. Words destroy as well as create. We may not be aware of the incredible power of words when we lash out in anger, make self-effacing statements or use back-handed humour. For better or for worse, our daily words leave a profound effect on others, and also affect us on a deep level of being.

When we become the initiates of higher consciousness, we are called to be mindful of our thoughts and our words. We understand that the world we live in is a product first of our thoughts, second of our words, and third of our deeds, for action always follows the intent of thoughts and words. First we think it. Then we say it. Then we act it. No war was ever fought without a build-up of invective. No relationship was ever ruined without a slash of razor-edged words.

Words are permanent. Once said, you can't take them back. You may think an apology will erase them, but they have become impressed upon consciousness, recorded in the ether of all time.

Every day we are challenged by stressful situations. How should we handle them verbally? Ask yourself the following questions:

One: Is what I am about to say true? We often make exaggerated or unfair accusations: 'You never...' 'You always...'

Two: Is what I am about to say necessary? Does it have merit? Or will it serve no purpose other than self-satisfaction?

Three: Is what I am about to say kind? This is where we often fall down. There are benevolent words we can choose that speak our truth, enable us to stand up for ourselves, defend ourselves, and right wrongs. Words of real strength do not destroy others.

St Josemaria Escriva once said, 'If you remembered the presence of your Angel and the angels of your neighbours, you would avoid many of the foolish things which slip into your conversations.'

In prayer, ask for the Angel of Words to help you be mindful of your words as the images of your soul. If you pray daily, you will naturally beautify your soul, and your words will naturally reflect that beauty. You won't have to stop and ask yourself those three questions. You will see a shift in what you say – and in your entire well-being.

MEDITATION

I centre myself in a comfortable position ... I focus attention on my breath, seeing it as light and energy which flows down from the Source through the crown of my head ... filling my body with radiance ... and flowing out through the soles of my feet ... so that I am connected to the inspiration of heaven and the grounding of the earth ... I then breathe in slowly three times ... one breath to relax more deeply and let thoughts and tension drain away ... one breath to centre my attention in stillness ... and one breath to expand my consciousness to the space around me.

I invoke with prayerful and loving intent the presence of my guardian angel and the Angel of Words, to share this journey with me ... assisting me with seeing things in new ways ... and inspiring me to take loving action in the world ... Now before me arise impressions of the Angel of Words ... I take a moment to observe ... and to give thanks for my partnership with the angelic realm.

I ask the Angel of Words to show me the past ... and how my words may have hurt others ... in criticism ... in anger ... in envy ... in carelessness ... I hear the words ... and when I hear them, I also see them ... as dark arrows that pierce the hearts of others ... and how others wither in their souls when the arrows strike ... I imagine how I would feel ... to be the one receiving those dark arrows ... The Angel shows me ... how hurtful words ... cast a cloud of unhappiness around me as well ... and how they diminish my own spiritual light.

I am presented with the opportunity ... to ask forgiveness ... and find redemption ... I express my sorrow and my regret ... and ask forgiveness for the times when my words have hurt others ... and when I do so, a light from heaven shines down upon me ... and I feel a healing take place deep within me.

I ask the Angel of Words to show me other times ... when my words have helped others ... in praise ... in love ... in encouragement ... in compassion ... I hear the words ... and when I hear them, I see them as streams of light which fall upon others ... as a dew nourishes the things that grow ... and I see how others brighten and glow in response ... I imagine how I would feel ... to receive the light of kind words ... The Angel of Words shows me ... how good words ... infuse my aura with brighter light ... which in turn attracts more positive things to me ... and sends healing energy out wherever I go.

I ask the Angel of Words to remain close by me ... in the chamber of my heart ... to help me choose the right words ... that will help and not hurt ... build and not destroy.

I take three measured breaths ... feeling the breath flow through my body ... reconnecting me to the present moment in time, space and place ... I give thanks to my guardian angel and the Angel of Words for the blessing of this experience ... and I return refreshed from my journey.

Appendix: On Finding Spiritual Teachers

In the course of spiritual growth, we may be inspired or led to study with particular individuals or schools. I am often asked for recommendations.

There are no universally good teachers who fit all needs; rather, there are many good and qualified teachers; you must find the one who is right for your needs. The teacher who works well for one person may not be suitable for another. The fit depends on the rapport between student and teacher, what the student needs, and what the teacher can provide. We are likely to benefit from multiple teachers as our growth progresses, and so we should not be reluctant to move on.

The saying goes that when the student is ready, the teacher will appear. We may meet a teacher or hear of one and feel drawn to that person. If we set our intent to be connected to the right teacher, and keep this focus in prayer, meditation and dreamwork, we will be guided appropriately. Timing takes its own course, and patience is sometimes required.

Don't be reluctant to experiment, sample and validate by taking courses, classes and workshops, and by having private readings/consultations. Pay attention to the feedback from your intuition. If things look good on the surface but don't feel right, move on. It may have nothing to do with the worthiness of the teacher, but simply how well you would get on together, and how much you would benefit. No matter how popular someone may be, if the fit isn't right for you, it simply isn't right, and trying to make it right will be unproductive.

Watch out for the 'I' word from teachers: 'I' this and 'I' that and 'I know' and 'I knew that.' Be especially cautious if you find them saying 'I knew that' after you've given information about yourself.

When it comes to readings and consultations, if a teacher tells you details about other people's problems and how he/she has solved/helped them, it means there is no confidentiality – for you as well. A session should be confidential; no exceptions. In some cases a reader/teacher might ask clients for permission to describe their cases in general terms as part of an example lesson for others – but private information should never be divulged.

Avoid those who emphasize the negative and constantly warn of bad things about to happen. Sometimes the tone of a teacher's message starts brightly and becomes progressively darker as the student becomes more involved and committed. Doomsayers can be very manipulative. Especially avoid anyone who predicts death. I once knew a self-described 'teacher' whose standard message to her female clients was that their partners were causing great problems, the women had to get away, they would die if they didn't, or their partners would die if they 'stood in the way'. Terrible damage can be done by this sort of irresponsible and unethical behaviour.

Many teachers work with spirit guides, and in the course of study you are likely to encounter one or more yourself. Stay well grounded and challenge guides in order to establish their credentials, for some entities masquerade and will waste your time. The well-intentioned entities expect to be challenged and do not mind. If they start telling you how important you are, be cautious. Also be wary of teachers who boast of having high-level 'secret' teachers.

Good teachers will aid your empowerment and not try to make you dependent on them. They will aid you in your discovery of your own wisdom and Truth. They recognize that at some point the relationship will be fulfilled and you will move on to other teachers.

These may seem like simple, obvious pointers. However, it's easy sometimes to give over too much power to a teacher or a spirit entity. You can always invoke the help of your guardian angel in matters of discernment. If you follow your guidance and your intuition, your spiritual study will be both enjoyable and fruitful.

A Miracle in Your Pocket

How to bring miracles into your daily life

- What are miracles?
- Do they really happen?
- And if so, how and why?

Both informative and inspirational, this little book draws on famous miracles from history and modern first-hand accounts to show you practical ways to bring 'miracle consciousness' into your own daily life. Miracles are not just for exalted saints and holy ones, but are products of a creative power we all have the ability to access.

Make
www.thorsonselement.com
your online sanctuary

Get online information, inspiration and
guidance to help you on the path to physical
and spiritual well-being. Drawing on the integrity
and vision of our authors and titles, and with
health advice, articles, astrology, tarot, a
meditation zone, author interviews and events
listings, www.thorsonselement.com is a great
alternative to help create space and peace
in our lives.

So if you've always wondered about practising
yoga, following an allergy-free diet, using the
tarot or getting a life coach, we can point you
in the right direction.

thorsons
element